CRACKERS & DIPS

CRACKERS & DIPS

MORE THAN 50
HANDMADE SNACKS

· · · · · · · · · · · · · · · · · · · ·

IVY MANNING

PHOTOGRAPHS BY
Jenifer Altman

CHRONICLE BOOKS
SAN FRANCISCO

ACKNOWLEDGMENTS

They say it takes a village to raise a child; the same could be said for a cookbook! I would like to thank my editor at Chronicle Books, Bill LeBlond, for hearing me out and seeing the potential in this project, and Sarah Billingsley for her always helpful and gracious guidance. Many thanks also to my grandmother Helen Zalubowski, for giving me her decades-old rolling pin and showing me how to use it, and to Chef Ian Titterton for sharing his vast baking knowledge with me. I also owe heaps of gratitude to my husband, Gregor Torrence, for discussing crackers and dips in depth for many, many hours. If patience is a virtue, he is a saint.

I would like to thank as well all of my friends and colleagues who were willing testers (and retesters) of the recipes herein. A special shout-out goes to my "kitchen angel," Rebecca Gagnon, a brilliant baker, DIY maven, and blogger (rcakewalk.blogspot.com) for her insights, enthusiasm, encouragement, and testing acumen. A mixing bowl full of gratitude also goes out to Sara Bir, Susan Gilbertson, Susan Theis, Heather Jones, Rosemarie Torrence, Danielle Centoni, Pam Henderson, Cathie Schutz, Deena Prichep, Michelle Smoody, Ryan Smith, and my best friend, Mamie Korpela, for giving me honest feedback and support in my little cracker journey. I owe you all a big bowl of cheese crackers!

INTRODUCTION

Wander down the snack aisle of the grocery store or peruse any specialty foods shop, and you'll find scores of crackers on the shelves, from preservative-laden fish-shaped snacks to elegant flatbreads with "Tuscan herbs." The average box of crackers can cost as much as a good cheese, but turn that box around and look at the ingredients list, and you'll find they're all made with the same simple, inexpensive ingredients: flour, oil, and salt.

The same question comes to my mind every time I see rows of pricey crackers in stores: Why would anyone spend that kind of money when all the ingredients you need to make your own better-than-boxed crackers are in your pantry right now? Homemade crackers are as easy to make as a batch of cookies, they are much tastier than mass-produced crackers, and they're great to give as a homemade gift. Perhaps the reason more people aren't making their own crackers is that there has never been a book to show home bakers how—until now.

As a dyed-in-the-wool snack tooth (the opposite of a sweet tooth), I've been making crackers for my family for years. In my work as a professional cook, catering chef, and culinary instructor, I have delighted clients with my homemade semolina cracker sheets, perfect garlic-rubbed crostini, animal crackers, and other crunchy treats. Clients and students alike have been amazed by how much more delicious homemade crackers are than the mass-produced, boxed kind, and they're especially thrilled when they learn how easy it is to bake crackers at home.

At the start of this book, I offer guidelines based on my years of experience and practice to help you learn simple techniques for rolling evenly thin dough, cutting crackers, and topping them like a pro, as well as tips and tricks for getting perfectly baked crackers that stay crisp for days. Once you get the hang of the basics of cracker craft, there are thirty-five recipes to try, from the Tangy Cheddar Cheese Crackers (page 21) we all grew up with to international snacks, like crunchy Senbei (Japanese rice crackers, page 39), that tap into our collective fascination with street food and snacks from afar.

8

Most of us are searching for healthful snack options, so I've included a chapter full of whole-grain and gluten-free crackers such as the addictive Flax Seed Pizza Crackers (page 68) and buttery Brown Butter–Hazelnut Crackers (page 63). There are also recipes that utilize some of the great new whole-grain flours that are making a splash in the baking world these days. Crackers like the Amaranth Crackers with Cheddar and Pepitas (page 70) and the Spelt Pretzel Rounds (page 59) prove that whole grains can be both healthful *and* delicious.

Since I know you're pressed for time now and then (or always), I have also included a collection of quick crackers and crisps that give you nearly instant snacking gratification. From the Pappadams Three Ways (page 84) to the Za'atar-Dusted Pita Chips (page 82), cracker making can be as quick and easy as punching a few buttons on the microwave or slicing up a bagel. And for the sweet-toothed, there's a chapter of dessert crackers like the Skinny Mint Chocolate Grahams (page 96) and the shatteringly crisp Cinnamon Pistachio Baklava Crisps (page 102).

Crackers by their very nature are made for dipping and topping, so I've included eighteen of my favorite dips, spreads, and schmears to give your homemade crackers the adornment they deserve. Some are deviously decadent (molten cheese fondue, anyone? See page 115.); others are virtuous and satisfying all in one bite (Wasabi Edamame Schmear, page 124). When appropriate, I suggest pairing the right cracker with a dip that accentuates the flavors and textures of both.

In a world of overprocessed snacks made increasingly less accessible by rising prices and less desirable because of their increased fat, sodium, and sugar content, *Crackers & Dips* will show you how to feed your snack cravings in a more delicious, healthful way, right from your very own kitchen.

TECHNIQUES FOR PERFECT CRACKER BAKING

For Good Baking, Measuring Accurately

Making crackers is easy, and it can be done with very few pieces of special equipment. That said, this is the part of the book where I'll get up on a soapbox and tell you the one thing I think you absolutely must have in your kitchen: a digital scale.

I do give both volume (cups) and weight (in grams, which is more accurate than ounces) measurements for ingredients in this book, but I strongly recommend you forgo the measuring cups for a digital scale. Why? Because 1 cup of flour can weigh between 115 to 155 grams depending on how compacted the flour is, relative humidity of the room, and how you put the flour in the cup.

Use a scale, and you won't have to worry about any of that, plus it's loads easier to add ingredients to the mixing bowl by weight as you work than it is to spoon them into those little measuring cups. Most digital scales have a "tare" button, so you can place your mixing bowl on the scale, press "tare" and it will zero out the bowl's weight. Then you can add the first ingredient, press tare, add the next ingredient, press tare, and so on, measuring all the ingredients in the same bowl without fussing with measuring cups. It makes baking easier, faster, and your results will more consistent. That's why pro bakers use scales and why an increasing amount of baking books are written with weights. Digital scales cost from relatively inexpensive for a basic model to highway robbery for a needlessly high-tech version. At the right price, a digital scale is an investment you can afford.

So you want to get into the delicious, crispy, crunchy world of cracker baking and you don't have a scale (yet)? You can measure the dry ingredients with measuring cups, but please follow this method: Fluff the dry ingredients in the bag or bin with a spoon, spoon the ingredient into the measuring cup until it is overflowing, and then, level the top with a butter knife. This procedure produces more consistent results than the "dip into the flour bin, scoop up the flour, and pour it into the mixing bowl" method.

Mixing and Working Ahead

For all the cracker recipes in this book, I offer the best method for mixing dough; for ease, I often use a food processor or stand mixer. Unless the machine method is absolutely the only way to proceed, I also offer an unplugged handmade method. In some

10

recipes, it doesn't make sense to dirty an appliance and it's just as easy to make the dough by hand. Such is the elemental simplicity of cracker making!

Once your dough is made, in many cases you can store it in the refrigerator for a few hours or up to a few days. I've indicated which crackers have good "do ahead doughs" in the instructions of the appropriate recipe. If you're not a habitual baker, parsing out the cracker making process into two parts can make the process feel easier, and just like cookies, fresh-baked crackers taste better right out of the oven, so working ahead has its advantages.

Rolling—There's More Than One Way To Thin A Cracker

The key to crackers with a crisp, crunchy texture is all in the rolling. Crackers that are too thick can break a tooth, ones that are rolled unevenly will bake unevenly, and crackers that are too thin will burn.

The very word rolling will conjure the image of a rolling pin in most minds. I do use a rolling pin for many of the crackers in this book, and later on we'll go over keys to success using a rolling pin, but I'd also like to introduce you to some tools and tricks for getting evenly thin dough, and thereby crisp crackers, that you may not have thought of.

GETTING THE THICKNESS RIGHT

Before we get into the different ways to roll the dough, let's talk about thickness. The thickness of your cracker dough will affect your baking times, cracker texture, and yields. That's why it's key to get your cracker dough the right thickness for each recipe. The most common measures for dough thickness in this book are ⅟₁₆ and ⅛ in/ 2 and 4 mm. To get a visual sense of what these measurements look like, pick up a penny. One U.S. cent is 0.0625 in/1.6 mm, or about ⅟₁₆ in/2 mm. To see what ⅛ in/4 mm looks like, stack two pennies.

Though the pennies give you a sense of what the appropriate thickness of dough looks like, it's a good idea to invest in one of the nifty rolling guide gadgets on the market to ensure your dough is evenly thin and of a precise thickness. My favorite rolling guide is a set of inexpensive plastic strips called Perfection Strips, available at kitchenware stores and online. They come in three color-coded measures (black: ⅟₁₆ in/2 mm; white: ⅛ in/4 mm; and red: ¼ in/6 mm), and when placed on either side of your cracker dough, the strips will serve as a guide to help you roll the dough evenly to your chosen thickness.

Another option is a set of rubber bands of varying thickness that stretch right onto your standard rolling pin (they don't work with tapered-end rolling pins); I like Regency's Evendough bands. The one drawback to the bands is that it is possible to roll over the dough with the bands, leaving unsightly indentations in the dough.

Barring the gadgets, a straightedge ruler made of washable material is a great tool for measuring thickness, length, and width of the dough as you are rolling it out, but it won't guarantee evenly rolled dough. I have a cheap, clear plastic ruler that lives in my gadget drawer and comes in handy nearly every time I'm making crackers.

ROLLING THE OLD FASHIONED WAY—WITH A PIN

The most obvious way to get your cracker dough into shape is to use a rolling pin. It's an effective, no-nonsense way to get that cracker dough thin, and it gives you a feel for the dough, which goes a long way in making you a great cracker-baker.

Start with a lightly floured surface and rolling pin: rub a few pinches of flour into your rolling pin, and then fling a few more pinches over a clean work surface. Place the dough in the center of the floured area and roll from the center of the dough away from you. Next, place the rolling pin back in the center of the dough and roll toward you. Resist the urge to roll back and forth over the dough; it's makes it difficult to get an even sheet of dough, and the back-and-forth motion actually toughens the dough.

After each complete stroke of the rolling pin, lift the dough and rotate and/or flip it to make sure it isn't sticking. If you need to, add flour, but only enough to insure the dough isn't sticking; adding too much flour will make the crackers overly dry. Keep rolling until the dough is the desired thickness.

In some cases where the dough has a well-developed gluten structure, the dough may spring back as your roll. If this happens, set the first bit of dough aside and start rolling out another piece of dough; the springy dough will relax after a few moments and will yield more easily.

Some of the higher-fat or wheat-free cracker recipes like Skinny Mint Chocolate Grahams (page 96) and Seeded Quinoa Crackers (page 66) have especially sticky doughs. In recipes like these, it's best to roll the dough between a sheet of parchment paper and a sturdy piece of plastic wrap. The nonstick surfaces keep the dough from sticking to the pin and the work surface, and it's easier to roll without adding lots of extra flour, which can change the texture of the final cracker.

PASTA MAKER

Pasta makers are designed to thin out pasta dough using a double roller system that is adjusted to progressively thinner widths. These machines (either hand-crank or stand mixer attachments are available) produce evenly rolled dough that can be made at just about any thickness, from ¼ in/6 mm to paper-thin. These inexpensive machines make great pasta, but they're also ideal for some sturdier cracker doughs as well. Using a pasta machine may seem daunting to the uninitiated, but it's quite fun, and you get the hang of it quickly; I've taught children as young as 4 years old to use a pasta machine like an old pro.

1. Break the cracker dough into manageable pieces (specified in each recipe where a pasta maker can be used). Shape the pieces into flattened disks and dust them with flour. Cover all but one disk loosely with plastic.

2. Feed the disk of dough through the pasta maker on the widest setting ("1" on most models). Dust the dough lightly with flour again, fold it in half, and feed it through the rollers on the widest setting again; this will help smooth the dough.

3. Adjust the pasta machine to the next setting (slightly thinner than the first). Fold the dough into the center of the piece of dough in thirds (as you would a letter), and feed the dough through the rollers with the open end leading, this will help make the edges cleaner on the ends, which is better for cutting neat-looking crackers.

4. Continue to feed the dough through the machine once on each setting, adjusting the roller to the next-thinner setting each time until the dough is as thin as directed in the recipe. If the dough becomes too unwieldy and long to handle, cut the dough sheet into more manageable lengths. Repeat with the remaining dough and cut the crackers as directed in the recipe. Save the scraps, this kind of dough can be re-rolled a few times.

Pressing

Some round crackers like the Senbei (page 39) and Smoked Almond Thins (page 62) are easiest to make thin not by rolling, but by pressing. Simply make small balls of the given dough, place them one at a

13

time between sheets of heavy plastic (a zip-top bag works well), and press down on the dough: it will spread into an even, wafer-thin round with almost no effort. You can use the bottom of a flat-bottomed dish (I use a crème brûlée dish) or a large juice glass to manually press out the dough, or smash the dough balls in a tortilla press. No matter how you press them, this method makes cracker making a breeze.

Slicing

Though most crackers in this book are all about thinness, there are a few recipes that rely on a chill-and-slice strategy, much like refrigerator cookies, for a crisp, crumbly texture. The secret to the crispness of Caesar's Sablés (page 48) and Irish Walnut and Blue Cheese Shortbread (page 55) is the shortness of their dough. They both contain a lot of fat; the fat coats the molecules of flour that in turn keeps long strands of gluten from forming, which makes for a crumbly, crunchy cracker similar to shortbread.

The best way to form these short dough crackers is to chill the dough in tight log shapes until the dough is firm. Once the dough is well chilled, it's easy to cut the dough into puck-shaped crackers using a sharp chef's knife and a sawing motion. Once baked, these crackers aren't thin, but they are melt-in-your-mouth crumbly with a nice crispness. An added bonus: short dough crackers can be made a few days ahead and sliced and baked whenever you're ready for hot, homemade crackers; always an impressive trick to pull out of your hat when you have guests.

Trimming, Cutting & Transferring

Once your dough is rolled out thinly, it's time to cut the crackers and get them on baking sheets. I use a dual-wheel pastry cutter that has both a flat wheel and a beveled one to give the edge of my crackers that appealing zigzag look (think saltines). A pizza wheel will work, too, but they tend to be larger than the little pasta/pastry cutting wheels you can pick up at any kitchen store. You do not want to use a sharp knife like a paring knife to trim your edges and cut your crackers because the blade will damage your work surface, silicon baking mats, and baking sheets.

Start by trimming the irregular edges of the rolled-out dough so that you can wind up with attractive, evenly cut crackers; they will look more professional, and it will make it easier for you to fit more crackers on the sheet pans. In most cases, the trimmed edges can

14

be re-rolled to make more crackers. On the other hand, if the rough-hewn edges don't bother you, and you'd like to embrace the rustic, homemade look, by all means leave those ragged edges in place.

Pick up the whole sheet of dough and transfer it to the baking sheet and you run the risk of stretching and deforming the dough, plus the crackers won't bake evenly if they're crowded on the baking sheet. On the flip side, cutting the crackers first and transferring them one-by-one to the baking sheet can be tedious, and it can disfigure the crackers. I found a happy medium for many recipes in this book: cut the rolled out dough into strips, transfer the strips to the baking sheet, and cut the strips crosswise into the desired cracker shapes. It makes making dozens of crackers much quicker, and the method allows for efficient use of baking-sheet space, with enough room around each cracker for them to brown evenly.

Topping & Docking

A well-topped cracker is a delicious cracker, but it makes no sense to sprinkle your crackers with gourmet finishing salt, seeds, or another topping only to have them tumble off the crackers once they're baked. That's why I'll remind you in the instructions to gently tamp down toppings with the bottom of a measuring cup or your fingers to adhere them to the cracker dough. When heavier toppings like the seed mixture on the "Everything" Flatbread Crackers (page 33) come into play, I use an egg wash (1 egg whisked with 1 tbsp water) to help adhere the seeds to the dough. Egg wash also lends crackers a dressy sheen once they are baked; so whenever you want an elegant cracker, don't forget your friend egg wash. Once you've made egg wash, you can keep it in an airtight container for a few days for future cracker batches.

As the crackers bake, steam trapped inside the dough will form, causing puffy spots in the crackers. To remedy this, you can use a baking technique called docking. By docking, or pricking each cracker with a fork or a wide tooth comb (that you use only for docking), you're allowing steam to escape from the little holes, so you'll have evenly baked crackers that have a level surface to slather with dips and spreads.

Baking

Since crackers are thin, they bake in minutes, not hours. This means that you need heavy duty baking sheets, a watchful eye, and a well-calibrated oven, or at least an oven whose quirks you are accustomed to. I use an oven thermometer placed in the center of the oven to check my oven temperature and make sure it's running true to the digital readout. That said, even the newest, most costly ovens have hot spots. That's why I instruct you to rotate baking sheets not just from back to front, but also switching the bottom sheet of crackers with the top sheet so that your crackers are evenly baked.

Even if you are a dough-rolling ace and your oven is dead-on in the temperature department, some crackers may be done before others on the same baking sheet. This especially happens in the corners and edges where the air circulation and temperature are higher. In each recipe, I provide both a baking time range and doneness cues like "brown around the edges" or "firm when poked." It's best to keep an eye on crackers as you're baking them to assess their progress, removing any that seem done, and letting others go longer in the oven if they need it. Use your senses, and your crackers will be wonderful.

Cooling & Storing

No one likes a limp cracker, so moisture is the most important thing to safeguard against in the realm of cracker making. When the crackers are done baking, transfer them immediately to a cooling rack that will allow air to circulate around the crackers. This important step prevents condensation from forming on the crackers, which might rob them of crunchiness.

Once the crackers are completely cool, store them in airtight, sealable containers in a cool, dry spot in your kitchen. As an extra insurance policy in humid climes and during rainy days, you may want to toss a food-safe desiccant packet (the kind you find in bottles of vitamins, jerky, and nori seaweed packets) in the container. The harmless Silica gel in these tiny packets will absorb excess moisture and keep your crackers crisp, but as the packets warn, the desiccant is not edible, so be sure to keep away from kids, and discard it after use.

Many of the crackers in this book keep well for days. I've indicated a "best by" time at the end of each recipe, but your mileage may vary depending on your atmospheric conditions. I've found that drier crackers, such as the Swedish Caraway Rye Crisps (page 43), and crackers that have a lot of sugar in them, like Rosemary Graham Crackers (page 98), can be kept for as long as three weeks, possibly longer if they are stored correctly.

16

THE CRACKER PANTRY

About 80 percent of good cooking is in the shopping. This mantra is especially true in cracker and dip making where the recipes are so simple. Please read through the following points about a few of the frequently used ingredients before you get started.

ALL-PURPOSE UNBLEACHED FLOUR

All-purpose wheat flour is a highly processed grain product that goes through several chemical processes including bleaching and bromating to make the flour lily-white. I opt for less-processed unbleached flour. It works exactly as well as bleached flour, without added chemical processes.

BARLEY MALT SYRUP

A common ingredient in baking and beer making, barley malt syrup, sometimes called barley malt extract, is used in cracker recipes to add a touch of sweetness (it's half as sweet as sugar) and a rich, malt flavor. Made from barley that has been sprouted and roasted, barley malt syrup has the consistency of molasses and the flavor of a toasty, buttery grain. Eden makes my favorite barley malt syrup; find it with alternative sweeteners in natural grocery stores, or buy it online. Dark corn syrup can be used in a pinch, but it won't provide the same butter flavor.

BUTTER

I use unsalted butter. I'd rather add my own measure of salt to recipes, rather than have the dairyman decide how much salt goes into my cooking. I buy organic butter because the flavor is noticeably better.

CRÈME FRAÎCHE

Crème fraîche [krehm FRESH] is a thick, velvety fermented dairy product that's common in Europe, where it's used in everything from pastries to dips and sauces (it can be boiled without curdling). Though it's similar to sour cream, it's generally thicker, higher in butterfat, and has a tangier, more complex flavor. You can find it at most grocery stores, but it tends to be costly. I recommend you make it yourself; see instructions on page 118.

17

NONHYDROGENATED SHORTENING
Many packaged crackers are made with hydrogenated or partially hydrogenated fats; these solid-at-room-temperature fats are cheaper than butter and give crackers a light, flakier texture. Because these chemically altered fats have been linked to elevated risk of coronary heart disease, they have become a pariah in the food world, and justly so. Spectrum Organics and Earth Balance have recently intro- duced nonhydrogenated shortening products made from organic palm oil. These products contribute the same texture to crackers as hydrogenated shortenings, but without the trans fats. Look for nonhydrogenated shortening in natural food stores.

OLIVE OIL
I use extra-virgin olive oil. Nothing fancy is necessary for the oil added to cracker doughs, but when it comes to dips and spreads, investing in better-quality extra-virgin olive oil can make a big difference.

PARMESAN CHEESE
I'm talking about real, imported Italian Parmigiano Reggiano when I say "Parmesan cheese." For some recipes, I recommend freshly grated cheese, while in others where "freshly grated" is not specified, it's fine to use the finely pre-grated cheese from the grocery store, provided that it's true Parmigiano Reggiano.

SALT
I use two kinds of salt frequently in this book: Fine sea salt is ideal for mixing into dough; flaky kosher salt sticks to cracker dough splendidly as a topping. The two have very different volumes and they cannot be used interchangeably.

WHOLE-WHEAT FLOUR

Whole-wheat flour, unlike white flour, still contains the germ when it is milled. That means it has some natural oils in it, and those oils can go off. Give your bag of whole-wheat flour a whiff; if it gives off a pronounced sour note, discard it. I recommend buying whole-wheat flour in small quantities in bulk and storing it in your freezer.

XANTHAN GUM

Xantha-what? It sounds more like a sci-fi villain than a baking ingredient, but xanthan (ZAN-thuhn) gum is a crucial ingredient in gluten-free recipes for the springy quality it can lend to dough. Xanthan gum is an all-natural ingredient made from fermented corn sugar. It keeps indefinitely in a cool, dry place. Find it at most grocery stores in the natural-food or gluten-free section, or buy it online.

19

1

LIGHT AND CRUNCHY CLASSIC CRACKERS

TANGY CHEDDAR CHEESE CRACKERS

These crackers are very similar to those neon-orange boxed "cheese" crackers we all grew up with, but without the heaps of sodium. The tangy flavor comes from aged Cheddar cheese, chicken bouillon powder, and annatto paste (also called achiote paste), a soft, crumbly seasoning blend made from achiote seeds. Annatto can be found at Latino grocery stores and conventional supermarkets in the Mexican foods section, or buy it online. If you can't find annatto, add 1½ tsp mustard powder to the flour; the crackers won't have the same orange hue, but the savory-sharp flavor will be similar.

MAKES ABOUT 120 CRACKERS

1 tsp annatto, crumbled

7 tbsp/105 ml room-temperature (75°F/25°C) water

1 tsp active dry yeast

1½ cups/185 g unbleached all-purpose flour, plus more for rolling

½ tsp fine sea salt

½ tsp baking soda

2 tsp chicken bouillon powder or crumbled bouillon cubes

1 cup/55 g finely grated loosely packed sharp Cheddar cheese

¼ cup/50 g chilled vegetable shortening, preferably nonhydrogenated

Preheat the oven to 350°F/180°C/gas 4. Combine the annatto and water in a glass measuring cup and stir to combine; the annatto will turn the water a deep crimson color. Stir in the yeast and set aside.

In the bowl of a food processor or a large bowl, pulse or whisk together the flour, salt, baking soda, and bouillon powder until combined. Add the cheese and shortening and pulse or cut the fat into the flour using a pastry blender until it is in tiny pieces and the mixture looks like coarse cornmeal, 15 one-second pulses with a food processor. Gradually add the water mixture, pulsing or stirring with a fork until the dough just comes together.

····▶

21

Turn the dough out onto a lightly floured surface and knead until smooth, 15 strokes.

Divide the dough into two balls. On a lightly floured surface, roll out each ball of dough into a rough rectangle that is about 1/16 in/2 mm thick, picking up the dough occasionally and rotating it to make sure it's not sticking to the work surface. Using a crimped pastry wheel, trim any irregular edges away. (Scraps can be reserved and re-rolled once.) Cut the dough into 1½-in-/4-cm-wide strips and lay them ½ in/12 mm apart on the prepared baking sheets. Cut the strips crosswise into 1½-in/4-cm squares and prick all over with a fork or comb.

Bake the crackers, rotating the baking sheets once from top to bottom and from back to front, until they are firm when touched and beginning to turn light brown on the bottom, 15 to 17 minutes. Watch the crackers carefully as they bake; if some crackers begin to burn before others are done, transfer them to a cooling rack and return the undone crackers to the oven for a few moments. Transfer the crackers to a cooling rack and cool completely before storing them in an airtight container. They will last for up to 1 week.

CRACKER TIP: This recipe can be made with any semi-firm cheese, so it's a great way to use up any odd bits of Swiss, provolone, or Gouda you have knocking around in the refrigerator.

22

A SCHOOL OF GLUTEN-FREE FISH CRACKERS

These crackers have the same great cheesy flavor as the Tangy Cheddar Cheese Crackers on page 21, but these are a lot easier to digest for people who don't do so well with wheat. They are actually so crisp and delicious, I guarantee you'll love them even if you're not living wheat-free!

The list of ingredients for this and other wheat-free recipes seems daunting at first, but as awareness of gluten intolerance increases, it's becoming much easier to find alternative flours in regular grocery stores. I keep a separate airtight container of my gluten-free flour in my pantry and pull it out whenever I want an easy-on-the-tummy treat. The instructions here are for making goldfish-shaped crackers, but if you haven't the patience for that, these crackers are equally delicious cut into squares.

MAKES ABOUT 240 FISH-SHAPED CRACKERS

2 tsp gluten-free chicken bouillon powder

1 tsp annatto, crumbled (see headnote, page 21)

½ cup/120 ml room-temperature (75°F/25°C) water

1 tsp active dry yeast

1 cup/160 g sweet rice flour

6 tbsp/65 g potato starch (not potato flour), plus more for rolling

¼ cup/30 g tapioca flour

½ tsp xanthan gum

¼ tsp fine sea salt

½ tsp baking soda

1 cup/55 g grated loosely packed sharp Cheddar cheese

¼ cup/55 g unsalted butter, at room temperature

23

Preheat the oven to 375°F/180°C/gas 4. Line two baking sheets with silicone baking mats or parchment paper. In a large measuring cup, combine the bouillon powder, annatto, water, and yeast. Stir until the yeast and bouillon have dissolved; set aside.

....➤

In the bowl of a food processor, combine the rice flour, potato starch, tapioca flour, xanthan gum, salt, and baking soda and pulse to combine. Add the cheese and butter and pulse until the mixture is crumbly and the mixture resembles coarse cornmeal, 10 one-second pulses.

Remove the food processor lid and pour the water mixture evenly over the rice flour mixture. Pulse until the mixture comes together into clumps, 20 one-second pulses. Divide the dough into two balls, flatten into 6-in/15-cm disks, cover with plastic wrap, and refrigerate for at least 30 minutes and up to 3 days.

Allow the dough to sit at room temperature for 5 minutes. Dust a work surface with potato starch and roll one of the disks into a ⅛-in-/4-mm-thick rectangle, picking up the dough occasionally and rotating it to make sure it's not sticking to the work surface. Using a small 1-in/2.5-cm fish-shaped cookie cutter, cut the dough into crackers. Alternatively, use a pastry wheel or pizza cutter,

trim any irregular edges away (save the scraps), and cut the dough into 1-in/2.5-cm squares. Transfer the crackers to a baking sheet using a floured spatula or bench scraper and poke each cracker once with a toothpick. Gather up the scraps, rewrap in plastic wrap, and chill while rolling out the second ball of dough. Repeat with the remaining dough. (Scraps can be re-rolled once.) Bake, rotating the pans once from top to bottom and from back to front, until the crackers are golden brown on the bottom, about 20 minutes. Transfer the crackers to a rack and cool completely. Store in an airtight container at room temperature for up to 1 week.

CRACKER TIP: Find miniature fish-shaped cookie cutters at craft stores and online craft sites like Makin's Clay Company and Daiso; they are often made for children's clay craft projects.

25

SODA WATER CRACKERS
WITH ALDER SMOKED SALT

At a young age, my dad introduced me to the simple pleasure of munching on saltines topped with smoked oysters while watching baseball on TV. To this day, saltines strike a sentimental chord; perhaps it's their plain, calming straight-forwardness I admire. Making homemade soda water crackers might not seem worth the trouble, but I assure you that these flaky, crispy, slightly sourdough-flavored crackers are infinitely better than their store-bought cousins. Try them with seafood dips like the Trieste-Style Crab Gratin (page 136) or the Smoked Salmon Crème Fraîche Dip (page 118), or eat them as my dad would have, slathered with butter and topped with smoked oysters.

MAKES ABOUT 100 CRACKERS

¾ tsp active dry yeast

½ tsp sugar

¾ cup/180 ml warm (120°F/50°C) water, plus 2 tsp

1¾ cups/215 g unbleached all-purpose flour, plus 6 tbsp/50 g and more for rolling

½ tsp baking soda

¼ cup/50 g shortening (preferably nonhydrogenated)

1 tsp fine sea salt

1 cup/115 g unbleached pastry flour

Alder-smoked salt, for sprinkling

In the bowl of an electric mixer, combine the yeast, sugar, and ¾ cup/180 ml water. Set aside until the mixture is creamy-looking, 10 minutes. Add the 1¾ cups/215 g all-purpose flour and mix with the paddle attachment on medium speed until a sticky dough forms, 2 minutes. Scrape down the sides of the bowl, cover with plastic wrap, and set aside at room temperature for 24 to 36 hours.

In a small bowl, combine the baking soda and remaining 2 tsp water. Add to the mixing bowl along with the shortening and sea salt. Blend with a paddle attachment on medium-low

‹····►

speed for 30 seconds. Switch to the dough hook and add the remaining all-purpose flour and all the pastry flour. Knead on medium-low speed until the dough comes together into a smooth ball, 3 minutes. Turn the dough out into a lightly oiled bowl, cover with plastic wrap, and let the dough rise until doubled in size, 3 hours.

Preheat the oven to 450°F/230°C/gas 8. Line two baking sheets with a silicone baking mat or parchment paper. Divide the dough into four balls. Place one ball of dough on a lightly floured surface; cover the remaining dough with plastic wrap. Roll out the first ball of dough using a pasta maker or a rolling pin until it is ¼ in/6 mm thick. Lightly flour the dough, fold it into thirds as you would a letter, and continue to roll the dough out until it is ⅛ in/4 mm thick. If rolling by hand, pick up the dough frequently and rotate it to make sure it isn't sticking to the work surface, adding flour only as necessary to prevent sticking.

Using a scallop-edged pastry wheel or pizza cutter, trim any irregular edges (save the scraps),

and cut the dough lengthwise into 2¼-in/5.5-cm strips. Carefully transfer the strips to a baking sheet, spacing the strips ½ in/12 mm apart and trimming them to fit the sheet as necessary. Sprinkle the strips lightly with the smoked salt and gently tamp down the salt with the bottom of a measuring cup. Cut the strips crosswise to make 2¼-in/5.5-cm squares. Prick each cracker with a fork or a comb. Repeat the process to fill the second baking sheet.

Transfer the baking sheets to the oven and bake for 3 minutes, then rotate the pans from top to bottom and from back to front. Reduce the temperature to 400°F/200°C/gas 6 and continue to bake until the crackers are light brown around the edges, 5 to 8 minutes. Transfer to a cooling rack.

Return the oven to 450°F/230°C/gas 8 and repeat the process with the remaining dough and scraps. Once the crackers are cool, transfer them to an air-tight container and keep them at room temperature for up to 2 weeks.

CORN BREAD CRISPS

Think corn bread, then think corn bread made into crisp little diamonds, and you get the idea here. These are the perfect partner for the Tangy Roasted Tomatillo and Avocado Dip (page 110) or the Molten Black Bean and Chorizo Dip (page 115).

MAKES ABOUT 80 CRACKERS

1 cup/145 g yellow cornmeal

¾ cup/90 g unbleached all-purpose flour, plus more for rolling

1 tsp baking powder

5 tsp sugar

1 tsp fine sea salt

⅛ tsp cayenne pepper

6 tbsp/85 g chilled unsalted butter, cut into ½-in/12-mm chunks

¼ cup/60 ml chilled buttermilk

Preheat the oven to 375°F/190°C/gas 5. Line two baking sheets with silicone baking mats or parchment paper. In a food processor or large bowl, combine the cornmeal, flour, baking powder, sugar, salt, and cayenne; pulse or whisk to combine.

Add the butter and pulse or use a pastry cutter to cut the butter into the dry ingredients until the mixture resembles coarse cornmeal, 15 one-second pulses in a food processor. Add the buttermilk and pulse or stir just until the dough comes together.

On a lightly floured surface, knead the dough until smooth, about 5 strokes. Divide the dough in half and form each half into a small rectangle that is about 1 in/2.5 cm thick.

Wrap the dough in plastic wrap and chill for at least 30 minutes and up to 24 hours.

Place one piece of dough on a lightly floured surface, cover with plastic wrap, and roll the dough out until it is ⅛ in/4 mm thick. Use a pastry wheel or pizza cutter to cut the dough into 2-in/5-cm diamonds; reserve the scraps. With a lightly floured spatula or bench scraper, transfer the diamonds to the prepared baking sheets. Repeat the process with the scraps.

Bake until the crackers are golden brown on the bottom and dry to the touch, 15 minutes, rotating the baking sheets once from top to bottom and from front to back. Cool the crackers on a rack and store in an airtight container for up to 5 days.

29

Light and Crunchy Classic Crackers

RITZY PEANUT BUTTER SANDWICH CRACKERS

These are just like the packaged peanut butter crackers Mom packed in your lunch, but without all the chemicals and trans fats—plus they taste much, much better. The secret to these buttery crackers is barley malt syrup, a sweet, thick syrup made from sprouted barley that is used by bakers and brewers when a light, malty flavor is desired.

You can, of course, forgo the peanut butter filling and enjoy these buttery crackers solo or with a savory spread like Bacon and Caramelized Onion Jam (page 128). They're also smashing served alongside a big bowl of chili.

MAKES 25 SANDWICHES (50 CRACKERS)

For the crackers

4 tbsp/55 g chilled unsalted butter

2 cups/255 g unbleached all-purpose flour, plus more for rolling

2 tsp baking powder

2 tsp sugar

1 tsp fine sea salt

2 tsp barley malt syrup or dark corn syrup

1 tbsp vegetable oil

½ cup/120 ml water

1 egg beaten with 1 tbsp water

1 tsp kosher salt

For the peanut butter filling

¾ cup/190 g creamy peanut butter

3 tbsp unsalted butter, at room temperature

¾ cup/80 g confectioners' sugar, sifted

TO MAKE THE CRACKERS: Cut the butter into ¼-in/6-mm chunks and place in the freezer while combining the dry ingredients. In a food processor or large bowl, combine the flour, baking powder, sugar, and sea salt and pulse or whisk to combine. Add the butter and pulse or cut the butter into the flour using a pastry

····▶

cutter or your fingers until the butter is in tiny pieces and the mixture looks like coarse cornmeal, about 15 one-second pulses.

In a small bowl, whisk together the barley malt syrup, vegetable oil, and ½ cup/120 ml of the water, stirring to dissolve the malt extract. Gradually add the water mixture to the food processor or bowl, pulsing or mixing with a wooden spoon to combine. Gather up the dough into a ball, flatten into a disk, cover in plastic wrap, and chill for at least 1 hour and up to 2 days.

Preheat the oven to 400°F/200°C/gas 6. Line two baking sheets with silicone baking mats or parchment paper. Roll the dough out on a lightly floured surface until it is 1/16 in/2 mm thick, picking up the dough occasionally and rotating it to make sure it's not sticking to the work surface. Using a round scalloped cookie cutter, cut the dough into 2½-in/6-cm rounds; reserve the scraps.

Fill one baking sheet with crackers, spacing them about ½ in/12 mm apart. Brush the crackers lightly with the beaten egg and then prick the crackers several times with a fork (a spoke pattern adds visual appeal). Sprinkle the crackers sparingly with some of the kosher salt and bake for 4 minutes; rotate the pan from back to front. Reduce the oven temperature to 375°F/190°C/gas 5 and continue to bake until the crackers are light golden brown and firm to the touch, about 8 minutes. Transfer to a cooling rack.

Return the oven temperature to 400°F/200°C/gas 6 and repeat the process with the remaining dough and scraps, baking the crackers one baking sheet at a time.

TO MAKE THE FILLING: Place the peanut butter, butter, and confectioners' sugar in a medium bowl or the food processor used to make the crackers. Beat with a handheld mixer or process until the mixture is fluffy. Chill the filling for 30 minutes.

Spread the bottom side of half of the crackers with 1½ tsp of the peanut butter filling. Top each of the peanut butter crackers with another cracker, salt-side up, to create a sandwich. Store in an airtight container for up to 4 days.

"EVERYTHING" FLATBREAD CRACKERS

My favorite morning treat is an "everything" bagel festooned with onion, garlic, sesame seeds, poppy seeds, and caraway; I'm hooked on their intriguing mix of flavors and textures. These elegant little crackers are an homage to those bagels, with all the delicious bagel decorations parked on top of flaky, tangy crackers made with crème fraîche.

"Everything" Flatbread Crackers are great smeared with any creamy dip: the Cervelle de Canut (page 119) and the Smoked Salmon Crème Fraîche Dip (page 118) come immediately to mind.

MAKES 24 CRACKERS

2 tbsp fried shallots or dried onion flakes

2 tsp dried minced garlic

2 tsp sesame seeds

1 tsp poppy seeds

1 tsp caraway seeds

1 tsp sel gris or other granular sea salt

2 cups/255 g unbleached all-purpose flour, plus more for rolling

1 tsp light brown sugar

½ tsp baking soda

½ tsp fine sea salt

¼ cup/60 ml crème fraîche (see Dip Tip, page 118), or sour cream

2 tbsp extra-virgin olive oil

6 tbsp/90 ml water

1 egg beaten with 1 tbsp water

33

Preheat the oven to 350°F/180°C/gas 4. Line two baking sheets with silicone baking mats or parchment paper. In a small bowl, combine the shallots, garlic, sesame seeds, poppy seeds, caraway seeds, and sel gris; set aside.

In a food processor or large bowl, combine the flour, brown sugar, baking soda, and fine sea salt

····▶

Light and Crunchy Classic Crackers

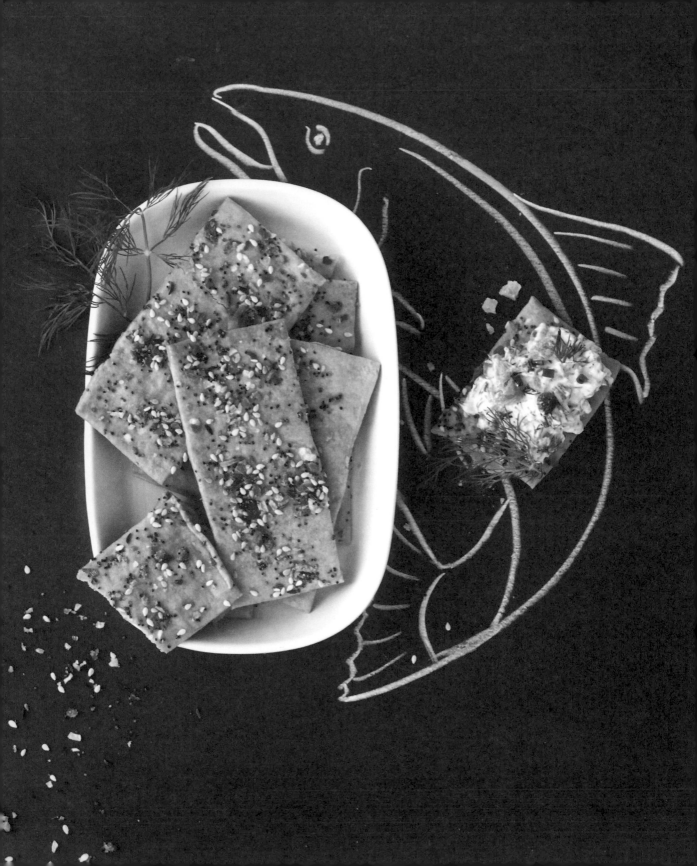

and pulse or whisk to combine. In a small bowl, whisk together the crème fraîche, olive oil, and water. Add the wet ingredients to the dry ingredients and pulse or stir with a wooden spoon until the dough comes together. Knead the dough by hand on a lightly floured surface until smooth, about 10 strokes.

Divide the dough into two balls, cover with plastic wrap, and let the dough rest for 30 minutes. Pat one ball into a small rectangle and roll it out on a lightly floured surface until the dough is $1/16$ in/2 mm thick, picking up the dough occasionally and rotating it to make sure it's not sticking to the work surface. Alternatively, use a pasta maker following the method on page 13 until the dough is $1/16$ in/2 mm thick, the number 5 setting on most machines.

Using a pastry wheel or pizza cutter, trim any irregular edges (save the scraps). Cut the dough into rectangles measuring 2 by 4 in/5 by 10 cm and transfer them to the baking sheet, spacing them very close together. Repeat the rolling and cutting process with the remaining ball of dough and scraps, using a second baking sheet.

Brush the crackers lightly with the beaten egg and sprinkle them with the shallot mixture. Using a flat-bottomed measuring cup, gently tamp down the toppings into the dough to adhere. Prick each cracker 4 or 5 times with a fork or comb.

Bake until the crackers are golden brown and crisp, 15 minutes, rotating the baking sheets once from top to bottom and from back to front while baking. Cool on racks and store in an airtight container for up to 5 days.

35

GARDEN OF EDEN VEGETABLE CRACKERS

My all-time favorite cracker growing up was the tangy, salty crackers studded with dehydrated vegetables, cut out into vegetable-like shapes. I've sorted out how to re-create the veggie-flecked crackers at home, with lots less sodium, sugar, and fat but all the savory flavor I remember. They may not be health food, but they are addictively delicious!

For the dehydrated vegetables in the recipe, I use the chunky bits lurking at the top of Knorr Vegetable Recipe Mix pouches. You can also buy dried vegetable blends in bulk at natural foods stores (sometimes labeled "soup vegetables"), or make your own blend with dehydrated bell peppers, dried onion flakes, and sun-dried tomatoes.

MAKES ABOUT 80 CRACKERS

2 tbsp dehydrated vegetables (see headnote)

1 cup/130 g whole-wheat flour

1 cup plus 2 tbsp/145 g unbleached all-purpose flour, plus extra for rolling

1 tbsp sugar

1½ tsp baking powder

2 tsp fine sea salt

½ tsp sweet paprika

2 tsp granulated onion powder

1 tsp granulated garlic powder

¼ cup/60 ml extra-virgin olive oil

½ cup plus 1 tbsp/135 ml water

1 tbsp tomato paste

Kosher salt

Preheat the oven to 400°F/200°C/ gas 6. Using a clean spice grinder or a mortar and pestle, grind the dehydrated vegetables until they are fairly fine; pieces should not exceed ⅟₁₆ in/2 mm wide, or the crackers will be difficult to roll and cut.

In a large bowl, whisk together the dehydrated vegetables, whole-wheat flour, all-purpose flour, sugar, baking powder, sea salt, paprika, onion powder, and garlic powder. Add the olive oil and rub it into the flour mixture with your fingers until it is completely incorporated and the mixture is crumbly. In a small bowl, whisk together the water and tomato paste. Add the water mixture to the flour mixture and stir with a wooden spoon until just combined.

Turn the dough out onto a lightly floured surface and knead until smooth and slightly elastic, about 20 strokes. Cover the dough with plastic wrap and let it rest for 30 minutes. (The dough can be made ahead up to this point. Refrigerate the wrapped dough for up to 24 hours.)

Lightly dust a clean work surface and a rolling pin with all-purpose flour. Divide the dough into two equal-size balls. Roll out one ball of dough until it is 1/16 in/2 mm thick, picking up the dough occasionally and rotating it to make sure it's not sticking to the work surface and adding more flour as necessary. If the dough springs back as you are rolling, set it aside and start rolling out the second ball; this will allow the gluten in the first ball of dough to relax, thus making it easier to roll out.

Using a pastry wheel or pizza cutter, trim any irregular edges (save the scraps). Cut the dough into 2-in-/5-cm-wide strips. Transfer the strips to a baking sheet, spacing the strips 1/2 in/ 12 mm apart. Sprinkle the strips sparingly with kosher salt and use the bottom of a measuring cup to gently tamp it into the dough. Prick the strips all over with a fork or comb and cut the strips crosswise into 2-in/5-cm squares. Repeat with the remaining dough and scraps.

Bake until the squares are light brown around the edges and firm to the touch, 12 to 15 minutes, rotating the pans once from top to bottom and from back to front while baking. Watch carefully; these crackers go from perfectly done to burned very quickly. If some of the crackers are done before others, transfer them to a cooling rack and return the undone crackers to the oven for a few more moments. Cool the crackers and store in an airtight container for up to 1 week.

2

THE GLOBAL CRACKER: CRISPY SNACKS FROM AROUND THE WORLD

SENBEI
(JAPANESE RICE CRACKERS WITH FURIKAKE)

I love senbei, salty-sweet Japanese rice crackers, but they're a pricey addiction—authentic Japanese rice crackers can run three times the amount of a domestic box! After tinkering around in the kitchen, I have come up with a formula for my own senbei—a simple blend of cooked white rice, sweet rice flour, oil, and water. The dough is a snap to make in a food processor, and the crackers are thinned by pressing pieces of dough between sheets of plastic wrap, so you don't even need a rolling pin!

The dough is flavored with furikake, a Japanese condiment made from sesame and nori seaweed, available at Asian markets. I glaze the crackers with a sweet-salty blend of good-quality soy sauce and mirin (sweet Japanese rice wine) so they have the same authentic flavor that makes packaged senbei so very addictive.

MAKES 38 CRACKERS

1½ tsp premium soy sauce

1½ tsp mirin

¾ cup/120 g sweet rice flour

⅓ cup/40 g cooked white rice

¼ tsp fine sea salt

2 tbsp canola oil

¼ cup/60 ml water

2 tbsp furikake (see headnote)

Preheat the oven to 350°F/180°C/gas 4. Line two baking sheets with silicone baking mats or parchment paper. Combine the soy sauce and mirin in a small bowl and set aside. In a food processor, combine the rice flour, cooked rice, salt, and canola oil. Pulse until finely ground. With the machine running, slowly add the water and process until the mixture is crumbly, 30 seconds. Transfer the mixture to a large bowl, add the furikake, and knead to combine, adding a few drops of water, if necessary, to make a dough that clumps easily when squeezed. (The dough can be made ahead up to this point. Cover in plastic wrap and refrigerate for up to 3 days.)

••••➤

39

Split a small plastic sandwich bag down the side seams, keeping it connected at the bottom seam. Place a heaping 1 tsp dough between the sheets of the plastic bag and press with the bottom of a flat-bottomed dish or juice glass, or use a tortilla press, to create a 2½-in/6-cm disk; the dough will be very thin. Carefully peel the dough round away from the plastic and place it on a prepared baking sheet. Repeat with the remaining dough.

Bake the unglazed crackers until they are dry around the edges, 5 to 6 minutes. Flip the crackers with your fingers, using a spatula to help, and continue to cook until the crackers are dry and starting to brown around the edges on the second side, 4 to 5 minutes. Maintain the oven temperature.

Brush the tops of the crackers with the mirin-soy mixture. Return to the oven and bake until the crackers are lightly browned but not burned, 2 to 3 minutes. Watch carefully; the sugar in the mirin will burn if baked too long. Allow the crackers to cool for 15 minutes on a wire rack; they will crisp up considerably as they cool. Store in an airtight container for up to 1 week.

CRACKER TIP: If you are aiming to make the senbei gluten-free, be sure to check the furikake label; some brands of furikake contain wheat or gluten.

SWEDISH CARAWAY RYE CRISPS

I fell head over heels in love with dark, crisp rye crackers during a recent trip to Scandinavia. Every morning, my husband and I sat down with his gracious relatives who offered us hearty breakfasts of rye crisps topped with a tantalizing array of gorgeous smoked and pickled fish. It seemed an odd way to start the day at first, but we were quickly hooked. Now the *smørbrød* breakfast has become something of a weekend ritual in our house; there's nothing better than lingering over the newspaper while nibbling on gravlax, herring, cheese, and pickles mounded on crisp rye crackers.

These crackers keep really well, so I often make a double batch and give them as gifts, packed into decorative jars or boxes with a jar of Smoked Salmon Crème Fraîche Dip (page 118) or Fresh Artichoke Dip (page 112) alongside to decorate them.

MAKES 30 CRACKERS

1 cup/115 g dark rye flour

1 cup/125 g unbleached all-purpose flour, plus more for rolling

1 tsp baking powder

1 tsp fine sea salt

½ tsp ground caraway seeds

2 tbsp chilled unsalted butter, cut into ¼-in/6-mm cubes

½ cup/120 ml whole milk

1 tbsp molasses

1 egg beaten with 1 tbsp water

2 tsp caraway seeds

Preheat the oven to 400°F/200°C/gas 6. Line two baking sheets with silicone baking mats or parchment paper. In a food processor or large bowl, combine the rye flour, all-purpose flour, baking powder, salt, and ground caraway and pulse or whisk to combine. Add the butter and pulse or rub with your fingers until the butter is in tiny pieces and the mixture resembles fine cornmeal, 15 one-second pulses.

....➤

43

In a measuring cup with a spout, combine the milk and molasses and stir until the molasses has completely dissolved. Gradually add the milk mixture to the flour mixture and pulse or stir with a wooden spoon until the dough comes together into a ball.

On a lightly floured surface, knead the dough until smooth, about 25 strokes. The dough will be slightly sticky; add flour only as necessary. Divide the dough into two balls, cover with plastic wrap, and let the dough rest for 30 minutes. (The dough can be made up to this point and stored in the refrigerator, tightly wrapped, for up to 2 days.)

Run the dough through a pasta maker following the instructions on page 13 until the dough is about $1/16$ in/2 mm thick, the 5 setting on most pasta makers. Alternatively, pat one ball of dough into a small rectangle and roll it out on a lightly floured surface until the dough is $1/16$ in/2 mm thick, lifting the dough and rotating occasionally to make sure it's not sticking, and adding flour only as necessary.

Using a pastry wheel or pizza cutter, cut the dough into long 2-in-/5-cm-wide strips; reserve any scraps. Transfer the strips to a prepared baking sheet and repeat the process of rolling and cutting with the remaining dough and scraps.

Brush the crackers lightly with the beaten egg and sprinkle them with the caraway seeds. Using the bottom of a measuring cup, press down gently to adhere the seeds to the crackers. Prick the crackers with a fork or comb. Use a pastry wheel or pizza cutter to cut the strips crosswise into 4-in-/10-cm-long crackers.

Bake until the crackers are golden brown around the edges and no longer pliable, 12 to 15 minutes, rotating the baking sheets once from top to bottom and from back to front while baking. Watch carefully to make sure the crackers do not burn. Cool the crackers on racks and store in an airtight container for up to 3 weeks.

44

PAPER-THIN SEMOLINA CRACKER SHEETS

These elegant crackers are served in long, thin sheets in Italy, hence their name *carte di musica*, "sheet music." This simple recipe is essentially eggless pasta dough, with all-purpose flour giving the dough elasticity, and high-protein semolina flour (also called hard durum wheat flour) lending a rich, buttery flavor and an addictive snap. The dough must be rolled until it's very thin (nearly see-through) for the best results. I use a pasta machine to do the job. If you haven't got a pasta maker, the dough can easily be rolled out paper-thin with a rolling pin and a little elbow grease.

I serve these cracker sheets stacked in a basket, inviting guests to break off pieces with their fingers. You can also cut the dough into rectangles measuring 4 by 1½ in/10 by 4 cm if you prefer precut crackers. Because of their neutral flavor, these crackers would be great with any of the dips in this book—the Rosemary Cannellini Dip (page 114) and St. Jack's Chicken Liver Mousse (page 134) are excellent choices.

MAKES TWELVE 1-FT-/30.5-CM-LONG SHEETS

1 cup/125 g all-purpose unbleached flour, plus more for dusting

1 cup/170 g semolina flour

⅔ cup/165 ml warm water

½ tsp fine sea salt

1 tbsp extra-virgin olive oil

¾ tsp fleur de sel, or other coarse finishing salt (see Cracker Tip)

Combine the all-purpose flour, semolina flour, water, fine sea salt, and olive oil in the bowl of an electric mixer using the dough hook. Once the dough comes together, mix on medium speed until the dough is smooth and springy when stretched, 3 minutes. (Add a bit of flour if the dough is too sticky to handle, a bit of water if the dough is not coming together.) Alternatively, mix and knead the dough for 6 minutes by hand. Cover the bowl with plastic wrap and allow the dough to sit at room temperature for 1 hour. (The dough can be made ahead up to this point and stored in the refrigerator, still in the bowl, tightly covered with plastic wrap, for up to 2 days.)

Preheat the oven to 400° F/ 200°C/gas 6. Line two baking sheets with silicone baking mats

••••▶

The Global Cracker: Crispy Snacks from Around the World

or parchment paper. Divide the dough into six equal-size balls. Dust one ball of dough with all-purpose flour and flatten it into a disk about ½ in/12 mm thick. Run the dough through a pasta maker following the instructions on page 13 until the dough is about ⅟16 in/2 mm thick, the 5 setting on most pasta makers, or roll it out with a rolling pin.* You will have a long, thin sheet of dough about 2 ft/61 cm long. Cut the dough crosswise into two equal lengths and transfer them to one of the prepared baking sheets. Repeat with another ball of dough and the second baking sheet.

Sprinkle the crackers with the fleur de sel and use a flat-bottomed measuring cup to lightly tamp it down into the cracker dough. Bake the crackers until they are golden brown and crisp, about 10 minutes, rotating the baking sheets once from top to bottom and from back to front while baking. Watch carefully: they go from ghostly pale to burned in seconds. Repeat with the remaining dough to make ten more cracker sheets.

CRACKER TIP: The sky is the limit with toppings for these crackers; here are just a few ideas.

ROSEMARY SALT: 1 tbsp fresh rosemary leaves chopped with ¾ tsp coarse finishing salt, such as fleur de sel

SPANISH SMOKE: ½ tsp Spanish smoked paprika plus ½ tsp kosher salt

TRUFFLE SALT AND PEPPER: ½ tsp truffle salt plus ½ tsp coarsely ground black pepper

GOUDA AND THYME: ¼ cup/ 25 g finely grated aged Gouda cheese, 2 tsp finely chopped fresh thyme

If rolling by hand, prepare the dough for rolling by picking up a ball in both hands and pulling on either end of the dough, stretching and wiggling it until it is about 5 in/12 cm long. Allow the dough to rest briefly while stretching the other dough balls. Roll out each stretched piece of dough as thinly as possible (about ⅟16 in/2 mm thick) with a rolling pin, lifting the dough frequently and rotating it to make sure it isn't sticking, and adding a little flour if necessary.

CAESAR'S SABLÉS

Everyone loves Caesar salad. So what if you could fit all the savory, salty flavor of that brilliant salad into a little crumbly cracker? Caesar lovers everywhere, rejoice: here is your cracker!

These rich crackers are similar to the French pastry/cookies called *sablés* [sah-BLAY], which means "sandy," and as the name advertises, these crackers have a sandy, crumbly texture and they're very rich, thanks to an ample dose of lemon olive oil.

The dough can be made up to three days in advance, so they're perfect for entertaining; just slice and bake when needed. Try them with a dab of Warm Olive Tapenade with Preserved Lemon (page 130), eat them by the handful, or use them as a garnish for Caesar salads as a sort of overgrown crouton. Whatever the application, they're *très délicieux*.

MAKES 50 TO 60 CRACKERS

2 cups/255 g unbleached all-purpose flour

1 cup/115 g grated Parmesan cheese (firmly packed)

½ cup/120 ml lemon-infused olive oil, or extra-virgin olive oil

1 tbsp finely grated organic lemon zest

1 garlic clove, finely chopped

1 tsp fine sea salt

**1 tbsp chopped anchovies (about 6 small fillets)
or 1 tbsp anchovy paste (optional)**

¼ cup/60 ml water

½ tsp freshly ground black pepper

In a food processor or large bowl, pulse or mix the flour, cheese, olive oil, lemon zest, garlic, and salt until well combined and crumbly. Add the anchovies (if using) and water. Pulse or stir until the mixture becomes crumbly and begins to stick together, 15 pulses (do not overmix), stopping once to scrape the sides of the bowl.

Turn half of the dough out onto a 16-in-/40.5-cm-long piece of plastic wrap and squeeze and gently knead the dough to form it into an 8- to 9-in-/20- to

23-cm-long log that is about 1¼ in/3.5 cm in diameter. Roll up the log in the plastic wrap and roll on the work surface under your palms to make a uniform cylinder. Repeat with the other half of the dough and another piece of plastic wrap. Chill the logs in the refrigerator until firm, at least 2 hours and up to 3 days.

Preheat the oven to 350°F/180°C/gas 4. Line a baking sheet with a silicone baking mat or parchment paper. Unwrap the logs and use a sharp, thin-bladed knife to cut the logs crosswise into ⅛-in-/3-mm-thick slices using a gentle sawing motion. If any crumbly bits break off while slicing, press them into the cracker and shape with your fingers into a round. Arrange the slices 1 in/2.5 cm apart on the baking sheets and sprinkle them with the pepper. If any of the crackers were sliced too thickly, use your fingers to press them out until they are of the same thickness as the others.

Bake until the crackers are golden brown around the edges, 15 to 20 minutes. Rotate the pans once from top to bottom and from back to front while baking. Transfer the crackers to a cooling rack. Once cool, store the crackers in an airtight container at room temperature for up to 4 days.

49

NORWEGIAN HAVRE KJEKS
(SWEET-SALTY OATMEAL ROUNDS)

A few years ago, my husband, Gregor, did some sleuthing to find the Norwegian branch of his family tree. With old black-and-white photos and the help of Facebook, he found his fourth cousins on a remote island in the western part of Norway. After days of air travel, a long car ride, and two ferry trips, we finally arrived on the picturesque fishing isle of Espevaer (population 162), to learn that nearly everyone we met on the island was somehow related to him.

The loveliest and most hospitable relative was Bitten Garvik Dalva, a silver-haired septuagenarian with an amazing proclivity for baking. She served us tea with no less than three homemade cakes, three kinds of cookies, and two kinds of homemade crackers. Upon much urging, she graciously transcribed this recipe from her yellowed notebook of recipes. Both sweet and salty with a comforting oat flavor, these gems are as delicious topped with smoked salmon as they are dunked in a glass of milk.

MAKES 60 CRACKERS

1¼ cups/110 g instant rolled oats

1¼ cups/170 g unbleached all-purpose flour, plus more for rolling

¼ cup/50 g sugar

½ tsp baking powder

1 tsp fine sea salt

½ cup/115 g salted butter, melted

¾ cup/180 ml plain Greek yogurt

Fleur de sel for topping

50

In a large bowl, mix the oats, flour, sugar, baking powder, and fine sea salt until thoroughly combined. In a small bowl, whisk together the butter and yogurt; add it to the dry ingredients and mix with a wooden spoon until the dough comes together. Knead gently in the bowl until the dough is smooth. Divide the dough in half, form into two 1-in-/2.5-cm-thick disks, cover them in plastic wrap, and refrigerate for at least 2 hours and up to 1 day.

Preheat the oven to 375°F/190°C/gas 5 and line two baking sheets with silicone baking mats or parchment paper. On a lightly floured surface, roll one of the disks out until it is ⅛ in/4 mm thick, picking up the dough and rotating it to make sure it isn't sticking to the work surface. Use a 2½-in-/6-cm-diameter biscuit cutter or juice glass to cut out rounds of dough. Place the rounds on one of the prepared baking sheets and sprinkle sparingly with the fleur de sel. Bake the crackers immediately, rotating the baking sheets once from front to back while baking, until the crackers are golden brown around the edges, 15 to 20 minutes. Repeat the rolling and cutting process with the remaining disk of dough and scraps (scraps can be chilled and re-rolled once).

Transfer the crackers on a cooling rack and store in an airtight container for up to 1 week.

51

BLACK PEPPER TARALLI

I first came across these little snack loops—not quite a cracker, not quite a breadstick—in Puglia in southern Italy; they were great "pack food" for nibbling on endless train rides and meanderings through dark cobblestone streets. Taralli come in both sweet and savory flavors; my particular favorites are the slightly hot black pepper–flecked ones. They are often served with wine, into which the taralli are dipped. Because they are so sturdy, they're great dunked into gooey dips like the Sconnie Beer and Cheese Fondue (page 120) or the Trieste-Style Crab Gratin (page 136).

MAKES 56 LOOPS

2 tsp active dry yeast

¾ cup/180 ml warm (120°F/50°C) water

1 tsp sugar

½ cup/120 ml white wine

¼ cup/60 ml extra-virgin olive oil

2 cups/255 g unbleached all-purpose flour, plus more for kneading

1¾ cups/290 g semolina flour

2 tsp fine sea salt

2 tsp freshly ground black pepper

1 egg beaten with 1 tbsp water

In the bowl of a stand mixer, combine the yeast, warm water, and sugar and set aside for 10 minutes. Add the wine and olive oil to the bowl and stir to combine. In another bowl, whisk together the all-purpose flour, semolina flour, salt, and pepper. Add the dry mixture to the yeast and water mixture and stir with a wooden spoon until the dough comes together. Attach the dough hook and knead on medium speed until the dough is smooth and elastic, 3 minutes. Alternatively, knead the dough by hand on a lightly floured work surface for 6 minutes. Coat a large bowl lightly with cooking spray; add the dough, cover with plastic wrap, and set aside until the dough has doubled in size, 1½ to 2 hours.

....▶

53

Preheat the oven to 350°F/180°C/ gas 4. Line two baking sheets with silicone baking mats or parchment paper. Divide the dough into two balls. Keep one ball covered with plastic wrap, and divide the other ball into 28 smaller portions. Roll each portion into a 6-in-/15-cm-long rope. Join the ends of each rope and pinch the ends together to create a small doughnut-shaped ring. Lay the rounds on the baking sheets 1 in/2.5 cm apart. Repeat with the remaining ball of dough.

Lightly brush each ring with the beaten egg and bake until the rounds are deep golden brown and crisp all the way through, 45 to 50 minutes. Rotate the baking sheets once from top to bottom and from back to front while baking. Transfer the taralli to a rack and cool completely. Store in an airtight container for up to 2 weeks.

CRACKER TIP: The dough can be made up to 1 day in advance. Refrigerate the unrisen dough in a large bowl tightly covered in plastic wrap until ready to use. Add an additional 40 minutes to the rising time, if necessary, to make sure the dough has doubled in size.

54

IRISH BLUE CHEESE AND WALNUT SHORTBREAD

These rich crackers combine creamy Irish blue cheese, slightly tannic toasted walnuts, and just a little swish of whiskey.

MAKES 80 CRACKERS

1 cup/225 g unsalted butter, at room temperature

4 oz/115 g soft blue cheese, such as Cashel, rind discarded

⅓ cup/65 g sugar

¾ tsp fine sea salt

1 tbsp Irish whiskey

2¼ cups/285 g unbleached all-purpose flour

½ cup/125 g walnuts, toasted, coarsely chopped

In the bowl of a mixer fitted with the paddle attachment, beat the butter, blue cheese, sugar, and salt on medium-high speed until fluffy, 3 minutes. Scrape down the sides of the bowl, add the whiskey, and beat to combine. Add the flour and stir on low speed until the flour is just absorbed and the dough comes together in clumps, 20 seconds. Add the nuts and stir into the dough by hand.

Divide the dough equally between two pieces of plastic wrap and form each portion into a 9-in-/23-cm-long log about 1½ in/4 cm in diameter. Cover up the logs tightly in plastic wrap and roll them briefly under your palms to make smooth cylinders. Chill until firm, at least 2 hours and up to 3 days.

Preheat the oven to 350°F/180°C/gas 4. Line two baking sheets with silicone baking mats or parchment paper. Unwrap the logs and, using a sharp, thin-bladed knife, cut the logs into ⅛-in-/3-mm-thick rounds. Transfer to the baking sheets, spacing them ½ in/12 mm apart, and bake until golden brown around the edges, 18 to 20 minutes. Rotate the baking sheets once from top to bottom and from back to front while baking.

Transfer the crackers to a rack and cool to room temperature. Store in an airtight container at room temperature for up to 4 days.

MIDDLE EASTERN FALAFEL CRISPS

These crackers have nearly the same ingredients as falafel, right down to the chickpeas. In this case, I use chickpea flour (also called garbanzo bean flour, gram flour, or besan), a dense, pale yellow flour ground from dried chickpeas. Chickpea flour is available at well-stocked natural foods stores or online. Great by the handful, Falafel Crisps pair well with Spicy Red Lentil Dip (page 109) or Tzatziki (page 123).

MAKES ABOUT 50 CRACKERS

1 cup/105 g chickpea flour (see headnote)

¾ cup/90 g unbleached all-purpose flour, plus more for rolling

1 tbsp dried parsley

1½ tsp ground cumin

1 tsp garlic powder

½ tsp baking powder

½ tsp ground coriander

½ tsp onion powder

¾ tsp fine sea salt

¼ tsp freshly ground black pepper

Pinch of cayenne pepper

6 tbsp/80 ml extra-virgin olive oil

⅓ cup/80 ml water

1 tsp light corn syrup

1 tbsp sesame seeds

1 tsp coarse salt

56

In a food processor or a medium bowl, pulse or whisk together the chickpea flour, all-purpose flour, parsley, cumin, garlic powder, baking powder, coriander, onion powder, sea salt, black pepper, and cayenne.

Add 5 tbsp/75 ml of the olive oil to the flour mixture and pulse or stir with a fork until the mixture forms crumbs. In a small measuring cup, combine the water and corn syrup and stir until the syrup dissolves. Add the water mixture to the flour mixture and pulse or stir with a wooden spoon until the mixture comes together into a slightly sticky dough. Knead gently on a lightly floured surface until smooth, about 5 strokes. Wrap the dough in plastic wrap and allow the dough to relax for 30 minutes.

Preheat the oven to 375°F/190°C/gas 5. Line a baking sheet with a silicone baking mat or parchment paper. Divide the dough into two balls and roll each ball out on a lightly floured surface until it is ⅛ in/4 mm thick, picking up the dough and rotating it a quarter turn frequently to make sure it is not sticking. Add more flour to the work surface, if necessary. Alternatively, use a pasta maker and the method outlined on page 13 to roll the dough until it is ⅛ in/4 mm thick, the 4 setting on most pasta makers.

Using a pastry wheel or pizza cutter, cut the dough into rectangles measuring 2 by 1 in/5 by 2.5 cm and use a lightly floured spatula or bench scraper to transfer the crackers to the prepared baking sheets. Repeat the rolling and cutting with the scraps.

Sprinkle the crackers with the sesame seeds and coarse salt, and tamp down the toppings with the bottom of a measuring cup to adhere them to the crackers. Brush the crackers with the remaining 1 tbsp oil and bake until the crackers are golden brown and crisp to the touch, 12 to 15 minutes, rotating the pan once from back to front while baking. If some of the crackers are done before others, transfer them to a cooling rack and return the undone crackers to the oven for a few more moments. Cool on a wire rack and store in an airtight container for up to 1 week.

CRACKER TIP: What's the corn syrup doing in a savory cracker recipe? The small amount of invert sugar gives the crackers an attractive caramelized brown hue once baked.

57

3

HEALTHFUL SNACKS
AND WHEAT-FREE CRACKERS

SPELT PRETZEL ROUNDS

Spelt is an ancient grain related to wheat that has enjoyed a resurgence lately as bakers and consumers have become interested in whole grains. Nutty and slightly sweet, spelt flour gives these little pretzel-flavored crackers a healthy dose of fiber and protein, plus a depth of flavor you just can't get from white flour. Look for spelt flour in the baking aisle or bulk section of whole foods stores, or order it online.

Proper pretzels are boiled in a lye solution that gives them their characteristic sour flavor and dark color. Instead of boiling the crackers in this recipe, I brush them with a baking soda solution; this step gives these crackers a great snappy exterior and characteristic pretzel flavor that makes them perfect for dipping into the Sconnie Beer and Cheese Fondue (page 120).

MAKES 32 CRACKERS

½ cup/120 ml warm water

1½ tsp barley malt syrup

1 cup/135 g spelt flour, plus more for rolling

1 tbsp sugar

¼ tsp fine sea salt

2 tsp baking soda

1 egg beaten with 1 tbsp water

½ tsp large-grain flaky salt

Preheat the oven to 350°F/180°C/gas 4. Line two baking sheets with silicone baking mats or parchment paper. In a small bowl, combine ¼ cup/60 ml of the warm water with the malt syrup and stir to dissolve.

In a large bowl, whisk together the spelt flour, sugar, and sea salt. Add the water mixture and stir until the mixture comes together into a ball. Knead with a dough hook in a stand mixer for 30 seconds on medium-low speed, or on a lightly floured surface until the dough is smooth and slightly elastic, 30 strokes. Set aside, cover with plastic wrap, and let the dough rest for 10 minutes.

In a small bowl, combine the remaining ¼ cup/60 ml water with the baking soda and stir to dissolve. Divide the dough

····▶

59

into two balls. Roll each ball of dough into a 14-in-/35.5-cm-long rope and cut each rope into 16 equal pieces. Lightly dust a work surface and rolling pin (a small rolling pin with a tapered end works best here) with flour and roll out each piece of dough into a 2½-in-/6-cm-diameter round. Place the rounds on the prepared baking sheets and brush each round with the baking soda solution.

Brush the rounds lightly with the beaten egg, sprinkle with the flaky salt, and bake until deep golden brown and crisp, about 15 minutes, rotating the baking sheets once from top to bottom and from back to front while baking. Cool the crackers on a rack and store in an airtight container for up to 1 week.

SMOKED ALMOND THINS

These high-protein, gluten-free crackers are my favorite go-to when I've got the afternoon hungries. The smoked almonds add a subtle, sweet-smoky flavor, and the crackers' lightness gives them an air of elegance that makes them right at home at a dinner party or cocktail soirée. Serve them with Fresh Artichoke Dip (page 112) or Warm Olive Tapenade with Preserved Lemon (page 130).

MAKES 45 TO 50 CRACKERS

5 tbsp/55 g potato starch (not potato flour)

½ cup/80 g sweet rice flour

⅔ cup/100 g smoked almonds

¾ tsp fine sea salt

⅓ cup/75 ml water

1 tbsp sesame butter (tahini) or sugar-free almond butter

1 egg beaten with 1 tbsp water

Preheat the oven to 400°F/200°C/gas 6. Line two baking sheets with silicone baking mats or parchment paper. Split the sides of a small sandwich bag, keeping the seam at the bottom of the bag intact. Set aside. Place the potato starch, rice flour, almonds, and salt in the bowl of a food processor. Pulse until the almonds are finely ground, 30 one-second pulses. The mixture will begin to look crumbly. Add the water and sesame butter and process until the mixture begins to clump, 20 seconds.

Measure a level 1 tsp dough and place it between the sheets of the plastic bag. Using a tortilla press or a glass with a flat bottom, press the dough into a thin, 2¼- to 2½-in/5.5- to 6-cm round. Carefully peel the round from the plastic and transfer it to one of the baking sheets. Repeat with the remaining dough, spacing the rounds about ½ in/12 mm apart. Brush the crackers with the beaten egg.

Bake the crackers until they are light golden brown around the edges, 8 to 10 minutes, rotating the baking sheets once from top to bottom and from back to front. Transfer the crackers to a cooling rack and let them cool completely before storing in an airtight container for up to 5 days.

BROWN BUTTER—HAZELNUT CRACKERS

These rich crackers were a great favorite with my chief recipe tester, Rebecca Gagnon; she liked them so much that she continued to "test" them even after we were both happy with the recipe!

The secret to their ultra-nutty, rich flavor is in the browned butter. Cooking butter until the milk solids turn brown transforms butter into a sweet, nutty-tasting liquid fat, a perfect accompaniment to the hazelnuts in these gluten-free hazelnut crackers. Try them topped with crumbles of salty blue cheese such as Spanish Valdeón and a whisper-thin slice of ripe pear or a dab of Figgy Bourbon Conserve (page 127).

MAKES 75 SQUARES

2¼ cups/295 g hazelnuts

3 tbsp unsalted butter

2 eggs

1 tbsp sugar

1 tsp fine sea salt

Preheat the oven to 350°F/180°C/gas 4. Cut two pieces of parchment paper to fit your baking sheets. Place the nuts on an unlined baking sheet and bake until they are light brown, their skins have cracked, and they smell nutty, 10 to 15 minutes. Set the nuts aside to cool and maintain the oven temperature.

In a small sauté pan, melt the butter over medium-low heat. Once the foaming subsides, the butter will begin to brown. Continue to cook the butter, swirling the pan frequently, until the butter is light brown (the color of light brown sugar), about 45 seconds. Do not overcook the butter or it will give the crackers a burned flavor. Pour the butter into a small glass bowl and chill it for 10 minutes. Collect enough of the clear liquid fat to measure 2 tbsp and discard the dark solids. Whisk together the brown butter and the eggs in a small bowl and set aside.

Rub the nuts together in a clean dish towel to remove their papery skins; discard the skins. Place the hazelnuts, sugar, and salt in a food processor and pulse until the nuts look like fine cornmeal, about 45 one-second pulses. (Be careful not to overprocess

....➤

63

the nuts or they will begin to turn into nut butter.) With the machine running, gradually add the butter and egg mixture through the feed tube until the mixture comes together into a moist ball of dough. (You may not need all of the egg mixture.)

Divide the dough into two portions. Center one portion of the dough on a piece of parchment paper. With moistened fingers, form the dough into a rectangle measuring 4 by 6 in/10 by 15 cm, cover with a piece of plastic wrap, and roll the dough out until it is 1/16 in/2 mm thick, lifting up the plastic now and then to make sure there are no creases in the dough.

Remove the plastic wrap and transfer the dough on the parchment paper to a baking sheet. Using a pastry wheel or pizza cutter, cut the dough into 2-in/5-cm squares. Any unattractive or partial segments of the dough can be scraped up with a bench scraper and added

to the second ball of dough. Repeat the rolling and cutting process with the second ball of dough.

Bake the crackers until they are light brown around the edges and firm when poked, 12 to 15 minutes. Rotate the baking sheets once from top to bottom and from back to front while baking, and watch carefully the last few minutes—they can go from perfectly cooked to burned in a matter of seconds. If some of the crackers are done before others, transfer them to a cooling rack and return the undone crackers to the oven for a few more minutes. Cool the crackers on a rack and store in an airtight container for up to 2 weeks.

CRACKER TIP: Don't panic if you spy a layer of white foam forming on the crackers as they bake— this is from the natural fats in the hazelnuts heating up. The foam will settle back into the crackers as they finish baking.

65

SEEDED QUINOA CRACKERS

Quinoa (pronounced KEEN-wah) is harvested from an ancient Andean grass related to the goosefoot plant. It's considered a sacred grain by the Incas, and for good reason; it is an excellent source of protein and lysine. Quinoa flour has a strong, grassy flavor. If you prefer something milder, try millet flour, which is mild and buttery. Find quinoa and millet flours at natural food stores or online.

Try these nutritious crackers with a creamy dip or spread like the Fresh Artichoke Dip (page 112) or (Don't Tell Them It's Vegan) Mushroom and Cashew Pâté (page 132).

MAKES 30 CRACKERS

1 tbsp hulled sunflower seeds

2 tsp unhulled toasted sesame seeds

1½ tsp flax seeds

1½ tsp fennel seeds

¾ cup/90 g quinoa flour or millet flour, plus more for rolling

½ cup/65 g cornstarch

½ cup/40 g freshly grated Parmesan cheese

¼ cup/30 g almond flour (or ¼ cup plus 1 tbsp/30 g blanched almonds, ground in a food processor)

1½ tsp baking powder

½ tsp xanthan gum

½ tsp fine sea salt

3 tbsp extra-virgin olive oil

6 tbsp/90 ml whole milk or soy milk

1 egg beaten with 1 tbsp water

Preheat the oven to 350°F/180°C/gas 4. Line two rimmed baking sheets with parchment paper or silicone baking mats. In a small bowl, combine the sunflower, sesame, flax, and fennel seeds.

In a large bowl, whisk together the quinoa flour, cornstarch, cheese, almond flour, baking powder, xanthan gum, and salt. Add the olive oil to the dry ingredients in the bowl and mix with a fork or your fingertips until the mixture looks crumbly and streusel-like. Add the milk and stir until the dough comes together. Knead the dough in the bowl until it is smooth and cohesive, about 5 strokes.

Divide the dough into two balls. Dust a large piece of parchment paper with quinoa flour and place one ball of dough on it; pat the dough into a small rectangle. Cover with plastic wrap and roll the dough out between the sheets until it is ⅛ in/4 mm thick, lifting up the plastic now and then to make sure there are no creases in the dough. Remove the plastic wrap and, using a pastry wheel or pizza cutter, trim any irregular edges (save the scraps). Cut the dough into

rectangles measuring 2 by 3 in/5 by 7.5 cm and transfer the crackers to the prepared baking sheets using a lightly floured spatula or bench scraper, spacing the crackers closely together.

Brush the crackers with the beaten egg and sprinkle them with the seed mixture, pressing gently with the bottom of a measuring cup to adhere the seeds to the crackers. Repeat the process with the second ball of dough, scraps, and the topping.

Bake the crackers until they are golden brown, 15 to 18 minutes, rotating the baking sheets once from top to bottom and from back to front while baking. Cool the crackers on a rack and store in an airtight container for up to 5 days.

CRACKER TIP: I prefer unhulled toasted sesame seeds for the topping in this recipe because the unhulled seeds are crunchier and have a nuttier flavor than the tiny white hulled variety (the ones you see on top of hamburger buns). Look for unhulled toasted (or "roasted") sesame seeds at Asian markets and whole foods stores.

FLAX SEED PIZZA CRACKERS

The dough for these crackers is held together with flax seeds, which become slightly gelatinous when soaked briefly. That gelatin helps bind the ingredients together without gluten, while the sundried tomatoes, Italian seasoning, and aged cheese give them loads of "junk food" flavor, without any of the junk.

MAKES 40 CRACKERS

½ cup/75 g golden or regular flax seeds

⅓ cup/75 ml hot tap water

⅓ cup/55 g chopped oil-packed sundried tomatoes, plus 1 tbsp reserved oil

⅓ cup/25 g grated pecorino romano cheese

2 garlic cloves, chopped

4 large fresh basil leaves

1½ tsp Italian seasoning blend

1 tsp fennel seeds

1 tsp fine sea salt

¼ tsp freshly ground black pepper

¾ cup/80 g almond flour (or ½ cup plus 2 tbsp/80 g blanched, slivered almonds, ground in food processor)

½ cup/60 g chickpea flour

Preheat the oven to 325°F/165°C/gas 3. Cut a piece of parchment paper to fit your baking sheet. Place the flax seeds and hot water in the food processor bowl and let them soak until all the water has been absorbed and the mixture is gelatinous, 15 minutes.

Add the sundried tomatoes and oil, the cheese, garlic, basil, Italian seasoning, fennel seeds, salt, and pepper to the processor bowl. Process until the mixture it becomes a gummy batter, about 30 seconds, stopping a few times to scrape down the sides of the work bowl. Add the almond flour and chickpea flour and pulse until the mixture comes together into a sticky ball, 40 pulses.

Turn out the dough onto the parchment paper. With moistened fingers, form the dough into a square measuring 6 by 6 in/ 15 by 15 cm, cover with plastic wrap, and roll out the dough to an 11-by-6-in/23-by-15-cm rectangle about 1/16 in/2 mm thick, lifting up the plastic now and then to make sure there are no creases in the surface of the dough. (It's okay if the rectangle does not have perfect edges or if a bit of dough squishes out the side of the paper, reserve it for patching.)

Remove the plastic wrap and use the reserved scraps of dough to patch any empty edges or corners, pressing with damp fingertips to smooth the dough into shape. Using a pastry wheel or pizza cutter, cut the dough into 2-in/5-cm squares and transfer the dough on the parchment paper to a baking sheet.

Bake the crackers until the edges are firm to the touch and starting to brown, about 18 minutes, rotating the baking sheets once from top to bottom and from back to front while baking.

Remove the crackers that are firm from the baking sheet and transfer them to a cooling rack. Break up the still-pliable, underdone crackers with a spatula and space them evenly on the baking sheet. Return the baking sheet to the oven and bake the remaining crackers until the edges begin to brown and the crackers are firm to the touch, 8 to 10 minutes more. Once cool, store the crackers in an airtight container for up to 1 week.

69

AMARANTH CRACKERS
WITH CHEDDAR AND PEPITAS

I was first introduced to amaranth flour through friend and fellow Portland baker Kim Boyce. In her excellent book *Good to the Grain*, Kim uses amaranth flour to add a rich flavor to her hazelnut cookies; one bite and I was instantly in love with this gluten-free flour.

Here, I pair amaranth flour with the bold Southwestern flavors of chili powder, cumin, and garlic and top the crispy crackers with Cheddar and hulled pumpkin seeds *(pepitas)*. Try them dunked in bold dips like the Tangy Roasted Tomatillo and Avocado Dip (page 110) or the Sconnie Beer and Cheese Fondue (page 120).

MAKES 35 CRACKERS

1 cup/105 g amaranth flour

½ cup/65 g cornstarch, plus 2 tsp for rolling

1 tsp baking powder

2 tbsp sugar

1 tbsp chili powder

2 tsp ground cumin

1 tsp fine sea salt

½ tsp garlic powder

¼ cup/60 ml water

3 tbsp extra-virgin olive oil

¼ cup/30 g pumpkin seeds *(pepitas)*

½ cup/50 g grated tightly packed Cheddar cheese

· · · · ▶

Preheat the oven to 375°F/190°C/ gas 5. Line two baking sheets with silicone baking mats or parchment paper. In a large bowl, whisk together the amaranth flour, cornstarch, baking powder, sugar, chili powder, cumin, salt, and garlic powder. In a small bowl, whisk together the water and olive oil. Add the wet ingredients to the dry ingredients and stir with a wooden spoon until the mixture forms a crumbly dough, about 10 strokes. Knead and squeeze the dough in the bowl until it comes together into a smooth ball. (If the dough seems a bit crumbly and dry, add a sprinkle of water to bring the dough together.)

Dust a piece of parchment paper with 1 tsp of the remaining cornstarch. Place the dough on the paper and pat it into a rectangle measuring 4 by 6 in/10 by 15 cm. Dust the dough with the remaining 1 tsp cornstarch. Cover the dough with a piece of plastic wrap and roll out the dough until it is 1/16 in/2 mm thick.

Remove the plastic wrap on top, trim the edges of the dough, and cut the dough into rectangles measuring 2½ by 1½ in/ 6 by 4 cm. (Save and re-roll the scraps.) Using a bench scraper or spatula, transfer the crackers to the prepared baking sheets, spacing them closely together. Sprinkle the pumpkin seeds and cheese over the crackers, pressing firmly to adhere the seeds and cheese to the dough.

Bake until the crackers are browned at the edges and crisp to the touch (underdone crackers will be quite pliable when you try to bend one), 14 to 15 minutes, rotating the baking sheets once from top to bottom and from front to back while cooking. When the crackers are completely cool, transfer them to an airtight container for up to 5 days.

72

MACADAMIA NUT AND COCONUT FLOUR CLUB CRACKERS

Coconut flour has become the rock star of the baking world as of late, thanks to its high fiber content (there are 5 g of fiber in just 2 tbsp), relatively high protein content, and mild, slightly sweet flavor. You won't be able to taste the coconut in this buttery cracker, just a rich, mild flavor reminiscent of Keebler Club crackers. An added bonus: these gluten-free beauties keep well, so they make great gifts for anyone trying to avoid wheat. Try them with the Fresh Artichoke Dip (page 112), the Bacon and Caramelized Onion Jam (page 128), or slices of artisanal cheese.

MAKES 35 TO 40 CRACKERS

¾ cup/120 g sweet rice flour

½ cup/80 g macadamia nuts

¼ cup/30 g coconut flour

½ tsp baking powder

½ tsp fine sea salt

½ tsp garlic powder

¼ tsp xanthan gum

3 tbsp chilled unsalted butter, cut into ½-in/12-mm pieces

2 eggs

Flaky salt

Preheat the oven to 350°F/180°C/gas 4. In a food processor, combine the rice flour, macadamia nuts, coconut flour, baking powder, fine sea salt, garlic powder, and xanthan gum. Pulse until the nuts are finely ground, about 30 pulses. Add the butter and pulse until the mixture resembles fine granola, 15 pulses. Add the eggs and process until the mixture comes together into a slightly sticky ball.

Form the dough into a rectangle measuring 5 by 6 in/12 by 15 cm that is about 1 in/2.5 cm thick and place it on a piece of parchment paper. Place a piece of plastic wrap on top of the dough and roll the dough out until it is ⅛ in/4 mm thick, lifting the plastic from time to time to prevent creases from forming in the surface of the dough.

Transfer the dough on the parchment paper to a baking sheet and remove the plastic. Using a pastry wheel or pizza cutter, trim the edges of the dough to fit the baking sheet (scraps can be re-rolled to make another small batch of crackers). Cut the dough lengthwise into 1¼-in-/3.5-cm-wide strips and then crosswise into 3-in-/ 7.5-cm-long crackers. Sprinkle the crackers with the flaky salt and press lightly with the bottom of a measuring cup to adhere the salt to the crackers.

Bake until the crackers are light golden brown, about 20 minutes, rotating the baking sheet once

from front to back while baking. Keep an eye on the crackers; if some are beginning to brown too much before the others are done, transfer them to a cooling rack and return the undone crackers to the oven for a few moments. When the crackers are completely cool, transfer them to an airtight container for up to 10 days.

CRACKER TIP: Coconut flour is very dense and absorbs a lot of moisture; use too much, and it can make your baked goods too dry. Be sure to spoon coconut flour lightly into the measuring cup when measuring or, better yet, weigh it on a scale for a more precise measure.

4

QUICK AND CRUNCHY: EASY CRACKERS TO MAKE IN MINUTES

CRISPY WONTON TRIANGLES

I used to make these crispy little triangles at an upscale restaurant where they were served as a garnish for a fancy smoked fish salad. By mid-shift, I always had to make more because the kitchen staff nibbled on them incessantly, such was their irresistible crunchiness and nutty flavor. Thankfully, they're incredibly easy to make: just coat packaged wonton wrappers with egg wash and seeds and deep-fry them.

I think they have a natural affinity for fish, especially in raw applications like the Albacore Tuna Tartare with Hijiki (page 138); or try them with Asian-inspired dips like the Wasabi Edamame Schmear (page 124). Although you can store them for up to 2 days, they're at their crispy best within a few hours of cooking.

MAKES 48 CRACKERS

1 tbsp white sesame seeds

1½ tsp black sesame seeds

1 tbsp cornstarch

1 egg

24 wonton wrappers

Fine sea salt

Canola oil for deep-frying

Line two baking sheets with paper towels. In a small bowl, combine the white and black sesame seeds. In another small bowl, whisk together the cornstarch and egg.

Place the wonton wrappers on a cutting board or baking sheet and brush lightly with the egg mixture. Sprinkle with the sesame seeds and salt and tamp the seeds down firmly with the bottom of a measuring cup to adhere the seeds to the wontons.

Prick each square several times with the tines of a fork and then use a pastry wheel or pizza cutter to cut each square on the diagonal to make two triangle-shaped crackers from each wrapper.

Pour the canola oil into a small, heavy saucepan to a depth of 2 in/5 cm. Heat the oil over high heat until an instant-read thermometer or deep-fry thermometer reaches 350°F/180°C. (If you don't have a thermometer,

●●●●▶

place one sacrificial wonton in the oil; it should rise to the surface and turn light golden brown in about 10 seconds.)

When the oil has reached the right temperature, add a few triangles to the pan and fry, flipping them once while cooking, until they are the color of new copper, 20 seconds. Transfer the fried crackers to the paper towels. Fry the remaining wonton triangles in small batches of 2 or 3 crackers per batch, adjusting the heat as necessary to keep the oil at about 350°F/180°C. The crackers are best served the day that they are fried.

FRICO WITH BASIL

There are just two ingredients to these little Italian-style cheese crisps, but every time you serve them, you'll be pronounced a genius. Traditionally, frico are made with aged Asiago cheese in their home region of Friuli, Italy, but I've found that just about any hard, aged, dry cheese will make wonderful frico; you might try the recipe with aged Parmigiano-Reggiano, grana Padano, Gruyère, Manchego, or Gouda cheese. Keep in mind that the moister the cheese, the chewier the frico, and the drier the cheese, the more crisp your crackers will be.

I add a fresh basil leaf to the center of each cracker before I bake them, but you can also garnish these little cocktail nibbles with a pine nut or walnut, as your fancy or pantry demands. Serve these rich cheese rounds with glasses of Prosecco (Italian sparkling wine) or on top of salads that need a little salty crunch.

MAKES 14 WAFERS

1 cup/60 g finely grated hard cheese (see headnote)

14 small fresh basil leaves

Preheat the oven to 400°F/200°C/gas 6. Line two rimmed baking sheets with silicone baking mats or parchment paper, cutting the paper so that it fits perfectly into the pans. Measure level table-spoonfuls of the cheese and space them 2 in/5 cm apart in little mounds on the prepared sheets. Gently press a basil leaf into the center of each mound of cheese.

Bake until the cheese has spread out and become lacy looking and the edges have begun to turn golden brown, 5 to 8 minutes, rotating the pans once from top to bottom and from back to front during baking. Watch carefully; if some crackers are beginning to brown too much before the others are done, transfer them to paper towels and return the undone crackers to the oven for a few moments.

Allow the frico to cool for 3 minutes on the baking sheets and then transfer them to paper towels to absorb any excess fat. Allow the frico to cool completely before transferring them to an airtight container. Frico can be kept at room temperature for up to 3 days.

CRACKER TIP: If you are a stickler for perfectly shaped crackers, use a round cookie cutter to coax the ragged edges of the cheese into a perfect circle while the baked crackers are still warm.

81

ZA'ATAR-DUSTED PITA CHIPS

I have to laugh when I see bags of pita chips for sale at the grocery store. All you have to do is cut pita bread into wedges, toss them with oil, and bake them! If only people knew how easy it is to make homemade pita chips, and how much better they taste than the greasy, salty bagged chips.

In this recipe, I sprinkle my homemade pita chips with *za'atar*, a Middle Eastern herb blend (in this case homemade) that is often mixed with olive oil and used as a bread dip. The dried savory, thyme, and tart sumac in za'atar give these chips an exotic flavor that is especially tasty when served with dips of a similar eastern Mediterranean ilk such as Tzatziki (page 123) or Spicy Red Lentil Dip (page 109). Although these chips keep for up to 3 days, it's best to reheat them briefly so they can regain some of their original savor.

MAKES 64 CHIPS

2 tsp dried savory

1 tsp dried thyme

2 tsp sesame seeds

½ tsp sumac

½ tsp kosher or flaky salt

4 pita bread rounds

¼ cup/60 ml extra-virgin olive oil

Preheat the oven to 350°F/180°C/gas 4. Using a mortar and pestle or clean spice grinder, grind the savory, thyme, sesame seeds, sumac, and salt until the mixture is finely ground and fragrant.

Cut each pita bread into eight wedge-shaped pieces and peel apart the layers to make two thinner pieces of bread out of each wedge. Arrange the wedges closely together in an even layer on two baking sheets. Brush the wedges with the olive oil and sprinkle with the ground spices.

Bake the chips until they are golden brown and crisp, 8 to 10 minutes, rotating the baking sheets once from top to bottom and from front to back and stirring the wedges while baking. Cool the chips on cooling racks before storing in an airtight container for up to 3 days. Reheat the chips in a 350°F/180°C/gas 4 oven for 4 minutes before serving after they have been cooled.

PAPPADAMS THREE WAYS

A *pappadam* (a.k.a. papad, poppadum, appalam) is a crisp, wafer-thin cracker made from ground lentils. In Indian cuisine they are often served as appetizers with little bowls of chutneys for dipping or as a crisp counterpoint to rich curries.

Pappadams come in fragile, brittle disks of about 15 per pack in either plain or seasoned varieties such as chile, cumin seed, or black pepper. My favorite brand is Lijat Papad—you'll know them by their peculiar label, showing a chubby boy and a possessed pink bunny inexplicably sneaking up behind him. Take care when transporting and storing the crackers; they shatter quite easily.

Pappadams can be cooked in a variety of ways, with each method lending a different flavor and texture to the crackers. Shallow-frying makes for a slightly larger, puffed cracker; microwaving them lends a crisper, slightly more oily mouthfeel; and toasting them over a gas flame gives them a smoky flavor and attractive charred edges. All the methods outlined here take a matter of seconds, so you can have these crispy snacks at a moment's notice. Serve them with Spicy Mint and Cilantro Chutney (page 126) or alongside your favorite curry.

EACH RECIPE MAKES 15 CRACKERS

SHALLOW-FRIED PAPPADAMS

¾ cup/180 ml vegetable oil

15 pappadams

Line a baking sheet with two layers of paper towels. In a 10-in/25-cm sauté pan, heat the vegetable oil over medium-high heat until moderately hot—a small piece of a pappadam dropped into the oil will puff and turn golden brown within a second. Add one whole pappadam and fry, flipping once with tongs, until tiny bubbles appear all over the cracker and it has puffed and begins to turn very light golden brown, 5 to 10 seconds. Transfer the cracker to the paper towels and continue the process with the remaining pappadams, adjusting the heat as necessary to avoid burning the crackers. Serve immediately or store in an airtight container for up to 1 day.

84

MICROWAVE PAPPADAMS

15 pappadams

2 tsp vegetable oil

Place two layers of paper towels in the center of the microwave. Lightly brush one side of a pappadam with the vegetable oil. Place directly on the paper towels in the microwave and cook on full power until the surface of the cracker is light golden brown in places and covered in tiny bubbles, about 1 minute. Repeat with the remaining pappadams. Serve immediately or store in an airtight container for up to 1 day. (Do not attempt to microwave the pappadams on a plate; the built-up heat will cause the plate to crack.)

TOASTED PAPPADAMS

15 pappadams

Turn on an exhaust fan or open a window. Hold one pappadam with tongs a few inches over a gas burner set to medium heat. Toast the pappadam, flipping and turning frequently so that the cracker is covered in tiny bubbles on both sides and is charred in places. Be careful not to ignite the cracker; keep moving it around so that it cooks evenly without burning. Repeat with the remaining pappadams. Serve immediately or store in an airtight container for up to 1 day.

85

GARLIC PUMPERNICKEL BAGEL CHIPS

These chips are inspired by the dark, delicious chips found in salty bagged snack mixes. They always seem to be the first thing picked out of the mix, and since they're as easy as slicing bread to make, I do it myself. If you can't find pumpernickel bagels, substitue light rye, plain, or any other savory flavor.

MAKES 80 TO 85 CHIPS

2 unsliced pumpernickel (or other savory flavor) bagels

2 tbsp vegetable oil

1 tbsp finely grated Parmesan cheese

1½ tbsp buttermilk powder (available in baking aisle)

2 tsp granulated garlic powder

1 tsp granulated onion powder

½ tsp freshly ground black pepper

½ tsp fine sea salt

Preheat the oven to 350°F/180°C/gas 4. Line two baking sheets with silicone baking mats or parchment paper. Using a sharp serrated knife, cut the bagels in half from the top down (not horizontally as you would if you were toasting the bagels). Slice the halves as thinly as possible into coin-shaped slices (ideally ⅛ in/4 mm thick or less) and place them in a large bowl. Toss with the vegetable oil until coated.

In a small bowl, combine the cheese, buttermilk powder, garlic powder, onion powder, pepper, and salt. Sprinkle the mixture over the bagel slices and toss gently until they are coated with the seasoning.

Arrange the bagel slices in a single layer on the prepared baking sheets, placing the thickest slices in the corners and the thinner slices in the center of the baking sheets. Press any excess coating on top of the slices. Bake until crisped, 8 to 12 minutes, depending on how thick the slices are. Cool on the baking sheets and store in an airtight container for up to 1 week.

VIETNAMESE SHRIMP CHIPS

Shrimp chips, also labeled shrimp or prawn crackers, are a popular snack in South-east Asia and parts of China. These foamy, crunchy crackers are made from potato or tapioca starch and dried shrimp. Sadly, many brands of shrimp chips don't have much shrimp in them at all and taste more like salty Styrofoam than anything from the sea, so be sure to buy ones that have dried shrimp in the ingredients list.

Since shrimp chips are shelf-stable, they're a great pantry staple for impromptu snacking or entertaining. All you need to do is heat some oil and these little multicolored pucks puff up into crunchy, impressive-looking snacks in seconds. I like to serve these with with a bowl of sweet chili sauce such as Mae Ploy for dipping.

MAKES 30 CHIPS

1½ cups/360 ml canola or peanut oil

2 oz/55 g shrimp crackers

Place the canola oil in a wok or small cast-iron pan and heat over high heat until hot but not smoking. (A deep-fat-frying thermometer will reach 350°F/180°C. If you don't have a thermometer, drop one shrimp cracker into the oil; if the oil is ready, the chip will puff and expand within 3 seconds.) Add four shrimp crackers to the oil at a time, and cook until they are puffed but not browned, 3 to 5 seconds, stirring and turning the crackers over in the oil so they cook evenly. Drain the fried crackers on crumpled paper towels and repeat with the remaining crackers, adjusting the heat as necessary to maintain the oil temperature. The crackers can be kept in an airtight container for up to 2 days.

87

CHEATER'S SESAME LAVASH

Lavash is a thin flat bread popular in the Middle East and Caucasus region, with its roots in Armenia. The bread is made in both a soft form that is used for sandwich wraps and a thinner, crisp lavash that is used as a cracker.

This "cheater" version of crispy lavash uses fresh, premade pizza dough instead of fiddling with yeast and kneading. Be sure to purchase the all-natural pizza dough found in the refrigerator case of better grocery stores; don't use the fatty dough that comes in a tube; it won't roll out thinly enough and will be far too greasy.

Lavash crackers are best the day they are made. They are especially welcome in a picnic basket or as part of a Mediterranean meze meal with the Rosemary Cannellini Dip (page 114) or the Spicy Red Lentil Dip (page 109). Any day-old crackers can be broken into pieces and used as croutons in salads or as a garnish for soup.

MAKES 12 ROUNDS

One 16-oz/450-g ball premade pizza dough

Unbleached all-purpose flour for rolling

2 tbsp unhulled toasted sesame seeds (see Cracker Tip, page 67)

Place a heavy rimmed baking sheet or a pizza stone on the center rack of the oven. Preheat the oven to 475°F/240°C/gas 9. Let the dough rest in its package at room temperature for 30 minutes.

On a lightly floured surface, divide the dough equally into four pieces. Divide each piece into three small balls to make twelve balls total. Cover all but one of the balls of dough with plastic wrap. Stretch out the uncovered ball of dough with your fingers into a small disk. Roll out the disk on the lightly floured surface with a lightly floured rolling pin (a taper-ended dowel-style rolling pin works best), picking up the dough after each stroke to make sure it isn't sticking. Roll out the dough as thinly as possible; you should be able to achieve an 8- to-9-in/20- to 23-cm circle. If the dough springs back when rolling, set it aside to let the gluten relax while you roll out another piece of dough. Alternatively, pick up the dough with your fingertips and gently stretch and wiggle the dough until it is as thin as you can get it without tearing; you should be able to get an 8-in/20-cm round with a bit of patience.

88

Spritz the dough with a little water, sprinkle with some of the sesame seeds, and gently roll over the dough with the rolling pin to adhere the seeds to the dough. Pull the oven rack halfway out of the oven, pick up the dough from one end, and carefully lay the dough on the hot baking sheet. It may stretch a little; an oblong shape is fine. Push the rack back into the oven and bake the lavash until it is browned in places, 3 to 6 minutes, depending on how thinly the dough was rolled. If the dough puffs up while it is baking, poke it with a fork to release the trapped steam. Use tongs to remove the lavash from the oven and place it on a cooling rack; it will crisp up as it cools.

Repeat the process with the remaining balls of dough. Once you get going, you can bake two rounds at a time while rolling out more dough. Store the lavash in an airtight container for up to 24 hours.

89

PERFECT CROSTINI

Crostini are fairly simple to make, yet I'm amazed by how often I come across sub-par examples of them. Every good cook should know how to make this most basic of kitchen staples, so here I give you the simple guidelines to make simply perfect crostini based on a method I've developed over years of catering gigs and thousands, possibly millions, of batches of crostini.

The most important thing is to start with the right loaf. Look for a rustic baguette that has a fairly fine crumb and a good, chewy crust, such as La Brea Bakery's French Baguette. Rubbing garlic all over the outside of the bread will lend the crostini a subtle garlicky flavor, and this is one of those times when it pays off to use your best olive oil.

MAKES 40 CROSTINI

1 garlic clove, peeled

One 1-lb/455-g baguette (see headnote)

2 tbsp extra-virgin olive oil

Kosher salt

Freshly ground black pepper

Preheat the oven to 375°F/190°C/gas 5. Rub the garlic all over the unsliced baguette; the surface will become slightly sticky and smell terrific. Discard the garlic clove or reserve it for another use.

Using a sharp serrated knife, cut the bread on a 40-degree angle into oblong slices that are about ¼ in/6 mm thick. Discard the first and last heel pieces, or nibble on them as you work. Arrange the crostini close together on a rimmed baking sheet. Brush the slices lightly with the olive oil (a dabbing motion is actually more effective), and sprinkle them with salt and pepper.

Bake until the crostini become light golden brown around the edges, 17 to 20 minutes, rotating the baking sheet once from front to back while baking. Watch carefully; do not let the crostini become too brown, because they will continue to crisp as they cool. Transfer the crostini to a wire rack and cool completely. Store in an airtight container for up to 5 days or freeze in zip-top bags for up to 3 months.

90

5

SWEET TREATS: DESSERT CRACKERS

ANIMAL CRACKERS
WITH ZESTY LEMON FROSTING

I loved animal crackers as a child, but as an adult, I find them to be overly sweet and bland at the same time. I've fixed that by developing my own recipe for animal crackers that uses less sugar than the boxed kind and features lemon zest in the cracker dough and a lemon glaze to decorate the crackers.

Oat flour lends a soft, milky flavor to these crackers that's strongly reminiscent of packaged animal crackers, so don't be tempted to leave it out. Oat flour is available in bulk at most natural foods stores and some grocery stores, but you can make your own by blitzing rolled oats in a food processor to a fine powder.

MAKES 45 ANIMAL CRACKERS

1½ cups plus 2 tbsp/200 g unbleached all-purpose flour, plus more for rolling

⅓ cup/40 g oat flour

¼ cup/50 g packed light brown sugar

¼ cup/50 g granulated sugar

2 tsp finely grated organic lemon zest, plus 1 tbsp freshly squeezed lemon juice

1 tsp baking powder

¼ tsp fine sea salt

4 tbsp/55 g chilled unsalted butter, cut into ½-in/12-mm pieces

¼ cup/60 ml buttermilk

2 tbsp honey

1 tsp vanilla extract

1¾ cups/180 g confectioners' sugar, sifted

1 tbsp milk

2 tbsp candy sprinkles (optional)

In the bowl of a food processor or a large bowl, pulse or whisk the all-purpose flour, oat flour, brown sugar, granulated sugar, lemon zest, baking powder, and salt to combine. Add the butter and pulse or use a pastry blender

····▶

93

or your fingers to cut the butter into the flour until the mixture resembles coarse meal, 15 pulses with a food processor.

In a measuring cup, combine the buttermilk, honey, and vanilla and stir until the honey has dissolved. Add to the flour mixture and pulse or stir with a wooden spoon until the dough just comes together. Remove the dough from the processor or bowl and knead gently on a lightly floured surface until smooth, 10 strokes. Flatten the dough into two equal-size disks, cover in plastic wrap, and chill them for at least 1 hour and up to 2 days.

Preheat the oven to 375°F/190°C/ gas 5. Line two baking sheets with silicone baking mats or parchment paper. Place one piece of the dough on a well-floured surface. Roll out the dough until it is ⅛ in/4 mm thick, lifting the dough and rotating to make sure it's not sticking to the work surface and adding all-purpose flour as necessary.

Use lightly floured cookie cutters to cut out animal shapes. Using a lightly floured bench scraper or offset spatula, transfer the cut-outs to one of the prepared baking sheets. Re-roll the scraps once and cut them out in the same way. Bake the animal crackers until light golden brown around the edges, 8 to 10 minutes, rotating the baking sheet once from back to front while baking. Cool the crackers on the sheet until they firm up, 5 minutes, and then transfer them to a wire rack to cool. While the first batch of crackers is cooling, repeat the rolling, cutting, and baking process with the remaining dough and scraps.

Once the cookies are completely cool, frost them. In a small bowl, combine the confectioners' sugar, lemon juice, and milk and stir until smooth. Spread a thin layer of the glaze over each animal cracker, scattering sprinkles over the crackers as you frost, if desired, and let them stand at room temperature until the glaze is completely set, 1 hour. Store in an airtight container for up to 1 week.

CRACKER TIP: To make your honey easier to measure, try microwaving it with the cap off until it is warm and more liquid in consistency; about 20 seconds on full power in the average microwave usually does the trick.

95

SKINNY MINT CHOCOLATE GRAHAMS

My husband is an absolute nut for chocolate-mint anything, so I came up with these to satisfy his Girl Scout cookie craving. I use a mixture of whole-wheat flour, unbleached all-purpose flour, and good-quality cocoa powder to give these crackers a sandy, crumbly texture and a deep, rich chocolaty flavor that's head and shoulders above any packaged chocolate-mint cookie.

The chocolate and mint combo and their long shelf life make these graham crackers a great gift for holiday giving; I like to sprinkle the tops of the crackers with crushed candy cane while the glaze is still wet, for an extra festive flourish.

MAKES 60 CRACKERS

14 tbsp/200 g unsalted butter, at room temperature

½ cup/100 g sugar

2 tbsp honey

1½ tsp peppermint extract

1½ cups/185 g unbleached all-purpose flour, plus more for rolling

1 cup/130 g whole-wheat flour

⅓ cup/30 g unsweetened cocoa powder

1 tsp baking soda

½ tsp fine sea salt

1 cup/170 g bittersweet chocolate chips

1 tsp canola oil

Preheat the oven to 350°F/180°C/gas 4. Line two baking sheets with silicone baking mats or parchment paper. In the bowl of an electric mixer or in a large bowl using a handheld mixer, beat the butter, sugar, honey, and peppermint extract together until fluffy, stopping occasionally to scrape down the sides of the bowl.

Sift both flours, the cocoa powder, baking soda, and salt into a medium bowl. Add the dry ingredients to the butter mixture and mix on low speed until the mixture forms moist crumbs; do not overmix. Gather up the dough with your hands (it will come together when squeezed), and divide the dough into two equal-size pieces. Form each piece of dough into a rectangle measuring 4 by 6 in/10 by 15 cm, cover in plastic wrap, and refrigerate for at least 30 minutes and up to 2 days.

Place a piece of parchment paper on a work surface and lightly dust it with all-purpose flour. Place a portion of dough on the paper, dust it with flour, and place a piece of plastic wrap over the dough. Roll the dough out until it is ⅛ in/4 mm thick, picking up the plastic once or twice to make sure there are no creases in the dough.

Cut the dough into the desired shapes using cookie cutters, and use a lightly floured spatula or bench scraper to transfer the crackers to one of the prepared baking sheets; reserve and chill the scraps. Prick each cracker a few times with a fork or comb and bake until they are crisp and smell chocolaty, 10 to 12 minutes, rotating the sheet once from front to back while baking. Transfer the crackers to a cooling rack.

While the first batch of crackers is baking, repeat the rolling and cutting process with another ball of dough; the chilled scraps can be re-rolled once.

In a small microwave-safe bowl or a double boiler, melt the chocolate chips until smooth. Remove from the heat and whisk in the canola oil. Using an offset spatula, spread about ½ tsp of the melted chocolate mixture over each cracker and place them on a baking sheet. Refrigerate the graham crackers until the glaze is set, about 30 minutes. Once the glaze has set, store the crackers in an airtight container in the refrigerator for up to 2 weeks.

CRACKER TIP: When baking crackers in batches, be sure to let the hot baking sheets cool for a few minutes before placing more raw crackers on them; if the raw dough is placed on hot baking sheets, it will spread and melt before the crackers are fully baked.

97

ROSEMARY GRAHAM CRACKERS
WITH S'MORES ACCOUTREMENTS

This recipe is adapted from a clever dessert served at Laurelhurst Market in Portland, Oregon, called The Night at Lost Lake. Chef de cuisine Shannon Preble serves these rosemary-flecked graham crackers with a brûléed marshmallow, a square of not-quite-melted chocolate, and a shot of whiskey. The subtle evergreen flavor of the crackers, combined with the other accoutrements, is a witty nod to the best grown up camping desserts.

    In this version, I put the whiskey in a gooey caramel sauce, so you can dunk your s'mores in a whiskey-tinged dip rather than drink the booze as a shot. Leftover crackers are killer good all by themselves, and they keep well for weeks, so they're the perfect cookie-jar filler.

MAKES 8 S'MORES PLUS 40 CRACKERS FOR SNACKING

For the grahams

⅓ cup/80 ml milk

2 tbsp honey

2 tbsp molasses

1½ tsp vanilla extract

1¾ cups plus 2 tbsp/245 g whole-wheat flour or 1 ¾ cups, plus 2 tbsp/255g graham flour (see Cracker Tip)

½ cup/60 g unbleached all-purpose flour, plus more for rolling

½ cup/100 g packed light brown sugar

¾ tsp baking powder

½ tsp baking soda

1½ tsp finely chopped fresh rosemary

1¼ tsp ground cinnamon

½ tsp salt

6 tbsp/85 g chilled unsalted butter, cut into ½-in/12-mm pieces

2 tbsp sugar

98

•••▶

For the salted whiskey caramel

¼ cup/50 g packed light brown sugar

2 tbsp heavy whipping cream

1 tbsp unsalted butter

1 tbsp light corn syrup

¼ tsp fleur de sel

1 tbsp whiskey

For assembly

One 4-oz/115-g bar 70 percent dark chocolate, broken into 1-in/2.5-cm squares

16 marshmallows

TO MAKE THE GRAHAMS: In a small measuring cup with a spout, whisk together the milk, honey, molasses, and vanilla until well combined; set aside. In a food processor or large bowl, combine the whole-wheat flour, all-purpose flour, brown sugar, baking powder, baking soda, rosemary, ¾ tsp of the cinnamon, and the salt and pulse or whisk to combine. Add the butter and pulse or use a pastry cutter to cut the butter into the flour mixture until it resembles coarse cornmeal.

Gradually add the milk mixture to the flour mixture and process or stir until the dough comes together. Gather the dough together and pat it into two 4-in/10-cm squares that are about 1 in/2.5 cm thick. Cover in plastic wrap and chill for at least 2 hours and up to 3 days.

Preheat the oven to 325°F/165°C/gas 3. Line two baking sheets with silicone baking mats or parchment paper. In a small bowl, combine the sugar and remaining ½ tsp cinnamon. Roll out one piece of the dough on a well-floured work surface with a floured rolling pin until the dough is ⅛ in/4 mm thick. The dough will be sticky; lift the dough frequently while rolling and dust with more flour, as necessary.

Working quickly, trim the edges of the dough and place the scraps in the freezer. Cut the dough into

2½-in/6-cm squares and use a floured bench scraper or spatula to transfer the crackers to one of the prepared baking sheets. Prick the crackers all over with a fork or comb and sprinkle them with about a third of the sugar-cinnamon mixture. As soon as the first sheet is filled, put it in the oven.

Bake, rotating the baking sheet once from front to back, until the crackers are browned and firm around the edges when poked, 12 to 15 minutes (the centers may still feel a bit soft and puffy; they will crisp up as they cool). While the first batch of crackers is baking, repeat the rolling and cutting process with the second ball of dough and the scraps. Transfer the baked crackers to a cooling rack and, once cool, store the crackers in an airtight container for up to 2 weeks.

TO MAKE THE CARAMEL: Combine the brown sugar, cream, butter, corn syrup, and fleur de sel in a small saucepan. Bring to a boil; reduce the heat to maintain a simmer and cook without stirring for 1 minute. Remove from the heat and carefully add the whiskey. Whisk to combine and keep warm over very low heat or store in a small thermos until ready to use.

TO ASSEMBLE: Preheat the oven to 275°F/135°C/gas 1. Place eight graham crackers on a baking sheet, top each square with a piece of chocolate, and bake until the chocolate just begins to melt, about 1 minute. Meanwhile, skewer the marshmallows with a metal pick and toast them carefully over a gas stove set to a medium flame or with a kitchen torch. Alternatively, broil the marshmallows on a foil-lined baking sheet until browned and gooey. Place two marshmallows on top of each chocolate-covered cracker, top with another cracker, and serve with the warm caramel on the side, for dunking.

CRACKER TIP: Graham flour is whole-wheat flour with a slightly coarser texture than regular whole-wheat flour. It gives these crackers a wholesome flavor and slightly more rustic texture, but whole-wheat flour will work, too.

101

CINNAMON PISTACHIO BAKLAVA CRISPS

I love baklava, the crispy, buttery Greek dessert made from layers of phyllo dough and nuts, but I seldom have the patience to layer and butter all those papery phyllo sheets. Halfway through the process, I'm ready to throw the stack of pastry out the window and hurl a few Greek curse words after it for good measure.

These little triangles are the answer to my baklava cravings and lack of patience. They have all the yummy goodness of Greek baklava compressed into just three layers of phyllo. They take minutes to put together and disappear just as fast.

MAKES 32 TRIANGLES

½ cup/70 g shelled unsalted pistachio nuts

2 tbsp sugar

¼ cup/55 g unsalted butter

¼ cup/60 ml honey

½ tsp ground cinnamon

¼ tsp fine sea salt

1 roll of 9-by-13-in/23-by-33-cm phyllo pastry sheets, defrosted

Preheat the oven to 350°F/180°C/gas 4. Cut two pieces of parchment paper to fit exactly into a baking sheet and a third sheet that is slightly larger. Place the nuts and sugar in a food processor and pulse until the nuts are very finely chopped, the consistency of cornmeal. Set aside. In a small microwave-safe measuring cup or a saucepan over low heat, melt the butter. Add the honey, cinnamon, and salt and whisk to combine.

Place one smaller sheet of the parchment paper on a work surface. Center one sheet of phyllo pastry on the paper. Keep the other sheets of pastry covered with a damp dish towel to keep them from drying out. Drizzle 1½ tbsp of the butter mixture over the phyllo sheet and then use a pastry brush to distribute the butter mixture evenly over the pastry. Sprinkle a generous 2 tbsp of the pistachio mixture over the pastry, and then top with a second sheet of phyllo, lining up the edges exactly to make a neat stack. Press down on the top sheet to adhere the layers.

·····▶

Repeat the process again, brushing the second sheet of phyllo with 1½ tbsp of the butter mixture and topping with 2 tbsp of the nut mixture. Place a third layer of pastry on top of the first two and press firmly to adhere the layers.

Transfer the stack of buttered phyllo pastry on the parchment paper to a baking sheet. Cover with the larger piece of parchment paper, and then place a baking sheet or inverted cooling rack directly on top of the phyllo stack to weigh it down. Bake until the dough is rich golden brown and crisp, 8 to 10 minutes, rotating the baking sheet once from front to back while baking and peeking after 8 minutes to check for doneness.

Remove the whole setup from the oven and let the pastry stack cool for 10 minutes with the baking sheet still on top of the pastry. (This weighted cooling time will keep the phyllo layers from coming apart when you're cutting them into triangles.)

Remove the top baking sheet and top parchment paper (reserve for the second batch), and transfer the phyllo stack on its bottom layer of parchment

paper to a cutting board. Using a sharp chef's knife, cut the phyllo stack in half lengthwise. Cut the stack crosswise four times to create eight squares, and then cut each square diagonally to create sixteen triangles.

Repeat the buttering and layering process with the remaining phyllo sheets, butter mixture, and nut mixture. Bake, cool, and cut as with the first batch, reusing the top piece of parchment paper when baking the second batch. (Refreeze unused phyllo sheets for another use.)

When the crisps are completely cool, transfer them to an airtight container. The crisps are best eaten within 1 day.

CRACKER TIP: Honey is the dominant flavor here, so this is a good time to splurge on single-flower honey. Experiment with local single-source honeys from your farmers' market; you'll be delightfully surprised at the difference between the commodity "honey bear" stuff and artisanal honey collected from carefully tended hives.

104

SPANISH OLIVE OIL TORTAS
WITH ORANGE-BLOSSOM WATER AND ANISEED

One of my guilty food pleasures is Spanish *tortas de aceite*—crisp olive oil crackers handmade in Seville. The tortas come individually wrapped in wax paper in sets of six, and are pretty pricey. Since I can blow through a stack of these in minutes, I decided it was time to figure out how to supply my habit in a thriftier manner. This recipe yields rich, flaky orange-anise Spanish tortas similar to the ones that tempt me at the grocery store, but they aren't nearly as greasy or expensive.

MAKES ABOUT 24 CRACKERS

7 tbsp/105 ml warm (120°F/50°C) water

6 tbsp/90 ml extra-virgin olive oil, preferably Spanish

2 tsp active dry yeast

Zest of 1 organic orange (about 1 tbsp)

1½ tsp orange-blossom water

2 cups/255 g unbleached all-purpose flour,
plus more for rolling

½ tsp fine sea salt

6 tbsp/75 g sugar

2 tsp aniseed

Preheat the oven to 350°F/180°C/gas 4. Line two baking sheets with silicone baking mats or parchment paper. In a small bowl, whisk together the warm water, olive oil, yeast, orange zest, and orange-blossom water.

In the bowl of a stand mixer or large mixing bowl, whisk together the flour and salt. Add the olive oil mixture and mix using the dough hook attachment on medium speed for 2 minutes or knead on a lightly floured surface for 5 minutes. Cover with plastic wrap and let the dough rise and relax in a warm place for 30 minutes.

Divide the dough into four equal-size balls. Dust a work surface and a rolling pin (a dowel-type tapered rolling pin works best) with flour and divide one ball of

••••➤

105

dough into six equal-size balls about the size of an unshelled walnut. Roll out the balls into 3½- to 4-in/9- to 10-cm rounds, picking up the dough and rotating it a quarter turn after each stroke so that the dough does not stick and the cracker will be an even round(ish) shape. If the dough springs back as you roll, let it rest and start rolling out a second small ball of dough. (As the first ball rests, the gluten will relax and it will be easier to work with.) Transfer the rounds to the prepared baking sheets and repeat with the remaining dough balls (you will need to bake the crackers in batches).

In a small bowl, combine the sugar and aniseed. Sprinkle a scant 1 tsp of the sugar mixture over each cracker and tamp down lightly with the bottom of a measuring cup. Prick the crackers all over with a fork or comb and bake until golden brown, about 15 minutes, rotating the baking sheets once from top to bottom and from back to front. Cool the crackers on racks and store in an airtight container for up to 5 days.

6

DIPS, SPREADS, AND SCHMEARS:
DELICIOUS WAYS
TO DRESS YOUR CRACKERS

SPICY RED LENTIL DIP

This spicy lentil dip is similar to ubiquitous hummus, but instead of using dried garbanzo beans, which require soaking and a long boiling time, I use red lentils. Red lentils don't need to be soaked, and they cook in a speedy 10 minutes. Because they are so much smaller than garbanzo beans, they also yield a smoother dip—silky smooth, in fact.

MAKES 2½ CUPS/600 ML

1 cup/195 g red lentils

1 bay leaf

Fine sea salt

2 tbsp freshly squeezed lemon juice

1 tbsp tomato paste

1 garlic clove, finely chopped

2 tbsp chopped cilantro leaves

2 tsp harissa

2 tsp ground cumin

2 tbsp extra-virgin olive oil

Rinse the lentils with cold water and drain. Combine the lentils, bay leaf, and 1 tsp salt in a medium saucepan. Add enough water to cover by 4 in/10 cm and bring to a simmer over medium-high heat. Reduce the heat to medium-low and simmer gently until the lentils are tender and falling apart, about 10 minutes. Drain the lentils in a fine-mesh sieve. Discard the bay leaf and let the lentils cool for 10 minutes in the sieve.

Transfer the lentils to a food processor and add the lemon juice, tomato paste, garlic, cilantro, harissa, cumin, and olive oil. Blend until smooth, stopping once or twice to scrape down the sides of the bowl.

Season the dip with salt, if desired, and transfer it to a serving bowl. Allow the dip to stand for at least 1 hour before serving to allow the flavors to develop. The cooled dip can be stored in the refrigerator in an airtight container for up to 1 week.

109

TANGY ROASTED TOMATILLO AND AVOCADO DIP

A little creamy, a little zesty, this is a nice alternative to the same old salsa from a jar. It's great with the Corn Bread Crisps (page 29), Amaranth Crackers with Cheddar and Pepitas (page 70), and, of course, tortilla chips. The flavor of this dip improves (and gets spicier) with time, so it's a great do-ahead dip for entertaining.

MAKES 2⅓ CUPS/555 ML

12 large tomatillos

1 Anaheim chile

6 garlic cloves, unpeeled

⅓ cup/5 g loosely packed chopped cilantro leaves

2 tbsp freshly squeezed lime juice

1 tbsp ground cumin

½ tsp sugar

½ sweet onion (such as Walla Walla or Vidalia), finely chopped

1 ripe Haas avocado, diced

Fine sea salt

Freshly ground black pepper

Adjust the oven rack so it is 6 in/ 15 cm below the broiling element. Line a rimmed baking sheet with aluminum foil and coat it lightly with cooking spray. Soak the tomatillos in a large bowl of hot tap water for 10 minutes. Drain, peel the papery skins from the tomatillos, and discard the skins.

Preheat the broiler. Place the peeled tomatillos, chile, and unpeeled garlic on the baking sheet and broil, turning the vegetables once with tongs, until the vegetables are lightly charred and have begun to collapse, 8 to 10 minutes.

Remove the baking sheet from the oven and when the chile is cool enough to handle, peel away the charred skins and remove the seeds and stem. Peel and discard the skins from the garlic. Finely chop the chile, garlic, and tomatillos or pulse in a food processor; the mixture should still be slightly chunky. Place the mixture in a serving bowl.

Add the cilantro, lime juice, cumin, sugar, onion, and avocado and stir to combine. Season with salt and pepper and allow the dip to stand at room temperature for 30 minutes to allow the flavors to meld. Keep in an airtight container in the refrigerator for up to 1 week.

DIP TIP: You can blend this dip without the avocado and whiz it in a blender to make an excellent enchilada sauce. It will make enough sauce to cover eight corn tortilla enchiladas.

111

FRESH ARTICHOKE DIP

This creamy, decadent dip is for true artichoke lovers, folks like myself who drool in anticipation of artichoke season every spring and fall and eat steamed artichokes (and nothing else) for dinner as soon as they come to market. This outstanding dip tastes nothing like the oily, flinty-textured dip recipes out there that use jarred artichokes. Instead, it tastes like true fresh artichoke hearts in all their buttery glory. It takes a little patience to trim the artichokes to get to the heart, but you'll get the hang of it quickly, and once you taste fresh artichoke dip, you'll never go back to the greasy, coarse recipes you've had in the past.

MAKES 1¾ CUPS/420 ML

1 lemon

2 artichokes

1 tbsp extra-virgin olive oil

1 shallot, finely chopped

2 tsp fresh thyme leaves, chopped

1 tsp finely grated organic lemon zest

½ cup/120 ml crème fraîche (see Dip Tip, page 118) or sour cream

¼ cup/60 ml mayonnaise

3 tbsp grated pecorino romano cheese

1 pinch cayenne pepper

Fine sea salt

Freshly ground black pepper

Fill a medium bowl with about 1½ cups/355 ml cold water and squeeze the juice of half of the lemon into the water. Using a serrated knife, trim the stalk of one artichoke to within 1 in/ 2.5 cm of its base. Saw off the top half of the artichoke leaves and snap off the remaining tough, dark green leaves around the outside of the artichoke until you reach the pale yellow cone of leaves in the center. Cut or pull off the pale yellow cone of leaves until you reach the fuzzy choke.

Using a sharp paring knife, trim away the tough green parts around the base and stem to get to the light green or white layer of the vegetable, rubbing the cut surfaces with the remaining lemon half to prevent discoloration. Quarter the artichoke heart and cut or scrape away and discard the furry choke from the heart. Chop the artichoke into ¼-in/6-mm pieces and quickly place in the lemon water until ready to use. Repeat the process with the remaining artichoke.

Drain the artichoke hearts. In a medium saucepan, heat the olive oil over medium heat. Add the artichoke hearts, shallot, and thyme and sauté until the vegetables are beginning to brown, 4 minutes. Reduce the heat to low and add ¼ cup/60 ml water. Cover and simmer gently until the artichoke is tender, 6 to 10 minutes, adding 2 to 3 tbsp water if the pan begins to look dry.

Mash the artichoke mixture with a potato masher until about half of the vegetables are mashed. Transfer to a medium serving bowl and allow the mixture to cool for 10 minutes. Add the lemon zest, crème fraîche, mayonnaise, cheese, and cayenne and stir to combine. Season with salt and black pepper. The dip can be made up to 2 days in advance and kept in the refrigerator, covered with plastic wrap, until ready to use.

113

ROSEMARY CANNELLINI DIP

Soaking and cooking dry cannellini beans makes this classic dip exceptionally smooth and flavorful. This dip is perfect with the Paper-Thin Semolina Cracker Sheets (page 45), Cheater's Sesame Lavash (page 88), and Black Pepper Taralli (page 53).

MAKES 3 CUPS/720 ML

1¼ cups/255 g dried cannellini beans

½ cup/75 g chopped onion

1 carrot, peeled and finely chopped

1 tsp dried rubbed sage

1 bay leaf

1 garlic clove, peeled

One 2-in/5-cm sprig of fresh rosemary

Fine sea salt

Freshly ground black pepper

2 tbsp extra-virgin olive oil

Place the cannellini beans in a large bowl; add water to cover by 2 in/5 cm and soak for 12 hours. Drain the beans and rinse them. Put the beans in a pot with the onion, carrot, sage, bay leaf, garlic, and enough cold water to cover by 1 in/2.5 cm. Bring to a boil, reduce the heat, and simmer until tender, 1 to 1½ hours. Add the rosemary sprig and ½ tsp salt, stir, and set aside for 15 minutes.

Drain the beans again, reserving 1 cup/240 ml of the cooking liquid. Pull the rosemary leaves from the stem and add them to the beans. Discard the bay leaf and rosemary stem. Transfer the beans and rosemary leaves to a food processor and process, adding a bit of cooking liquid if necessary, until the mixture is smooth. Season the dip with salt and pepper. Transfer the dip to a serving bowl, drizzle with the olive oil, and serve. To store, cool the dip completely in the refrigerator before sealing in an air-tight container for up to 4 days.

114

MOLTEN BLACK BEAN AND CHORIZO DIP

Every cook needs a great spicy bean dip in his or her repertoire, and this is mine. I start with canned black beans, give them a kick with chipotle chiles, and make the otherwise guilt-free dip "molten" by adding a layer of *queso blanco* (a mild Mexican melting cheese), with a smattering of sautéed chorizo sausage on the top. The resulting dip is a fiesta of textures and flavors, with just enough warm gooey cheese to qualify it as comfort food at its best. This dip begs to be attacked with Corn Bread Crisps (page 29) or tortilla chips.

MAKES 3 CUPS/720 ML

1 tsp cumin seeds

Two 15-oz/425-g cans black beans, drained and rinsed

½ cup/10 g lightly packed chopped cilantro leaves, chopped

2 green onions, chopped

3 garlic cloves, finely chopped

1 tbsp chopped canned chipotle chiles in adobo (see Dip Tip)

¼ cup/60 ml freshly squeezed lime juice

Fine sea salt

Freshly ground black pepper

1 cup/115 g grated *queso blanco* or Monterey Jack cheese

6 oz/170 g Mexican chorizo sausage, casings removed

Preheat the oven to 350°F/180°C/gas 4. In a small saucepan over medium heat, toast the cumin seeds until they are fragrant, 45 seconds. Grind the toasted cumin seeds using a mortar and pestle or clean spice grinder until they are a fine powder.

Place the black beans, cilantro, green onions, garlic, chipotle, lime juice, and cumin in a food processor and pulse until nearly smooth, stopping once to scrape down the sides of processor. Season with salt and pepper.

····▶

115

Transfer the bean mixture to a 4-cup-/940-ml-capacity oven-proof baking dish and cover with the cheese. In a small sauté pan, cook the chorizo over medium heat, stirring constantly, until cooked through and crumbly, about 10 minutes. Drain off the fat and sprinkle the chorizo over the top of the dip. Bake the dip until the cheese has melted and it is bubbling around the edges, 40 minutes. Serve hot.

DIP TIP: Chipotle chiles are smoked jalapeños packed in tomato purée. Be careful when handling them: unlike the rather innocuous raw jalapeño chiles grown these days, chipotles pack a real punch. It's a good idea to wear gloves when handling them.

117

SMOKED SALMON CRÈME FRAÎCHE DIP

You might not think the words *Norway* and *culinary tour* go together, but I went absolutely food-crazy when vacationing there. I was especially taken with the smoked fish, caviar, and rich crème fraîche that are served everywhere as part of the *smørbrød* open-face sandwich buffet tradition.

This simple dip is homage to the pure flavors of those Norwegian pig-outs. Since the dip is quite elemental, it's important to buy the best cold-smoked salmon you can get; I am partial to wild Alaskan salmon. Crème fraîche is inexplicably expensive in the United States, especially considering how easy it is to make at home! I've included a simple recipe in the Dip Tip.

MAKES 1¾ CUPS/420 ML

4 oz/115 g cold-smoked salmon slices

1 cup/240 ml crème fraîche

2 tbsp finely chopped fresh chives

**4½ tsp freshly squeezed lemon juice, plus
2 tsp finely grated organic lemon zest**

1 tbsp finely chopped fresh dill

1 tbsp drained capers

Ground white pepper

Fine sea salt

Finely chop the salmon into pieces that are no larger than ¼ in/6 mm square. In a medium bowl, gently fold together the fish, crème fraîche, chives, lemon juice, lemon zest, dill, capers, and ¼ tsp pepper. Refrigerate the dip for at least 1 hour to allow the flavors to meld. Season with salt and more pepper, if needed. Store in an airtight container in the refrigerator for up to 5 days.

DIP TIP: For 1 cup/240 ml crème fraîche, combine 1 cup/240 ml heavy whipping cream with 2 tbsp buttermilk in a glass jar or container. Cover with plastic wrap and let the mixture stand at room temperature until it is the consistency of thin sour cream, 12 to 24 hours. Whisk well and store in the refrigerator for up to 2 weeks.

118

CERVELLE DE CANUT

This tangy, creamy cheese spread means "brain of a silk worker" in French, but calm down, it's vegetarian! The dip originates in Lyon, France, where silk workers *(canut)* formed a large part of the working class in the eighteenth century.

This unique dip is delicious and simple; think Boursin, but with a college education. It's great on neutral-flavored crackers like the Paper-Thin Semolina Cracker Sheets (page 45), but it's zesty enough to stand up to highly seasoned crackers like the Middle Eastern Falafel Crisps (page 56).

MAKES ABOUT 1 CUP/240 ML

½ cup/120 ml *fromage blanc* (see Dip Tip) or puréed small-curd cottage cheese

½ cup/120 ml crème fraîche (see Dip Tip, page 118)

1 tsp freshly squeezed lemon juice, plus 1 tsp finely grated organic lemon zest

½ shallot, finely chopped

1 garlic clove, green sprout in center discarded (if present), finely chopped

1½ tsp fresh thyme leaves

1 tbsp chopped fresh chives

Fine sea salt

Freshly ground black pepper

In a medium bowl, combine the *fromage blanc*, crème fraîche, lemon juice, lemon zest, shallot, garlic, thyme, and chives. Season with salt and pepper. Cover with plastic wrap and refrigerate for at least 1 hour. Serve chilled. Store in the refrigerator in an airtight container for up to 1 week.

DIP TIP: *Fromage blanc* [froh-MAHZH BLAHNGK] is a fresh cheese with a loose, creamy consistency similar to farmer's cheese, but with very little, if any, fat. Find it at cheese shops and grocery stores in little tubs, or use blended small-curd cottage cheese instead.

119

SCONNIE BEER AND CHEESE FONDUE

You can take the girl out of Wisconsin (a.k.a. Sconnie), but you can't take the beer and cheese off her menu. I grew up in the lovely lakeside town of Sheboygan, Wisconsin, where beer and cheese are considered two of the major food groups. One of my favorite recipes from home is beer and cheese fondue. The proteins in the aged Cheddar and the acids in the beer and lemon juice in this recipe help to keep the fondue from separating, so it stays creamy and dippable for a few hours if you keep it warm in a fondue pot or electric mini–slow cooker.

Serve this dip with the Paper-Thin Semolina Cracker Sheets (page 45), apples, and grilled sausages for an elegant winter supper, or pair it as a snack with Spelt Pretzel Rounds (page 59) at your next party.

MAKES ABOUT 2 CUPS/480 ML

1 garlic clove, peeled and halved lengthwise

1 cup/240 ml lager or IPA beer

4½ tsp cornstarch

2 tsp freshly squeezed lemon juice

2⅔ cups/225 g grated extra-sharp Cheddar cheese,
at room temperature

1⅓ cups/115 g grated aged Gruyère cheese,
at room temperature

1 tbsp stone-ground (grainy) mustard

Rub a 2-cup/480-ml fondue pot or miniature slow cooker with the garlic. Place the garlic and ¾ cup/180 ml of the beer in a medium saucepan and bring to a simmer over medium heat. In a small bowl, whisk together the remaining ¼ cup/60 ml beer, the cornstarch, and lemon juice. Add the cornstarch mixture to the saucepan and cook, stirring frequently, until the mixture is thickened and bubbling, 3 minutes.

Remove the pan from the heat. Add a handful of the grated cheeses and whisk in a zigzag pattern until the cheese has melted. Return the pan to low heat and continue to add the remaining cheese in handfuls, stirring in a zigzag pattern and adding more cheese only once the last handful has melted.

Increase the heat to medium-low and cook, stirring constantly with a heatproof rubber spatula, until the mixture is smooth and *just* begins to bubble around the edges, about 5 minutes; the texture of the fondue will be slightly grainy if it is underdone (see Dip Tip). Do not let the fondue boil or simmer. Immediately remove the pan from the burner, stir in the mustard, and pour the fondue into the prepared warmer. Serve within 1 hour.

DIP TIP: If your fondue begins to separate, take it off the heat immediately and add 1 or 2 tsp lemon juice. Whisk thoroughly in a zigzag motion and return the mixture to low heat. If the fondue was not too far gone, it will return to its creamy glory.

If your fondue is slightly grainy on the tongue after you've added all the cheese, the cheese may not be fully melted yet. Continue to cook the dip over medium-low heat, stirring constantly, until it just starts to bubble around the edges; it will now be velvety smooth and ready to pour into the fondue pot.

121

TZATZIKI

I learned to make this creamy yogurt dip as an exchange student in northeastern Greece. I was placed with a family with two incredible cooks—my host father was a retired pastry chef and my host mother was a no-nonsense housewife who spent most of her time in the kitchen. Jackpot! The first thing I learned to make in their kitchen was this thick, garlicky tzatziki; it's been a staple in my repertoire ever since.

MAKES 3½ CUPS/340 ML

32 oz/960 ml whole-milk plain yogurt

1 cucumber

Fine sea salt

2 garlic cloves, halved lengthwise, green sprout discarded

2 tbsp extra-virgin olive oil

Stack two 1-ft/30.5-cm squares of cheesecloth and run them under cold water. Wring out the fabric and lay it in a fine-mesh sieve set over a medium bowl, allowing the excess cloth to hang over the sides. Pour the yogurt into the fabric, gather up the excess cloth, and tie them up with string. Place the setup (including the sieve and the bowl) in the refrigerator until the yogurt is very thick, about 3 hours.

Peel the cucumber, halve it lengthwise, and scoop out the seeds. Finely chop or grate the cucumber, place it in a small bowl, toss with 1 tsp salt, and place it in a fine-mesh sieve set over the sink to drain for 1 hour.

Scoop the yogurt out of the cheesecloth and place it in a medium serving bowl; discard the whey and cheesecloth. Rinse the cucumber, pat it dry with paper towels, and place it in the bowl with the yogurt. Finely chop the garlic and then use the side of a chef's knife to smash the garlic until it is a fine paste. Add the garlic paste to the yogurt and cucumber and stir well to combine. Season with additional salt and allow the dip to sit in the refrigerator for at least 2 hours to allow the flavors to develop. Drizzle with the olive oil immediately before serving. Store in the refrigerator in an air-tight container for up to 4 days.

123

WASABI EDAMAME SCHMEAR

The fresh, clean flavor of this thick soybean-based dip, or schmear, as I like to call it, goes well with the sesame seeds on the Crispy Wonton Triangles (page 77) and the soy and mirin flavors of the Senbei (page 39). It's even more virtuous served with thinly sliced carrots and blanched pea pods. The heat from the wasabi will intensify with time; so if you prefer just a whisper of wasabi, add it right before serving.

MAKES 1½ CUPS/360 ML

One 12-oz/340-g bag frozen shelled edamame (green soybeans), defrosted

⅓ cup/75 ml water

2 tbsp freshly squeezed lemon juice

2 tbsp sesame butter (tahini)

2 tsp wasabi paste (not powder)

Fine sea salt

2 tbsp vegetable oil

In the bowl of a food processor, combine the edamame, water, lemon juice, sesame butter, wasabi paste, and 1 tsp salt. Process until the mixture is smooth, about 4 minutes, stopping to scrape down the sides of the work bowl once or twice while blending. With the machine running, slowly add the vegetable oil and process until incorporated. Taste the dip and season with salt, if needed. Keep in an airtight container in the refrigerator for up to 1 week.

124

SPICY MINT AND CILANTRO CHUTNEY

This emerald-green dip mingles on the tongue with an appetizing balance of fresh minty flavor, tartness, sweetness, and a bit of heat. It's best to follow the recipe, let the chutney sit for an hour so the flavors have a chance to bloom, and then add additional chile, sugar, or lime if desired.

MAKES 1¼ CUPS/300 ML

½ cup/40 g dry, unsweetened coconut flakes

3 cups/40 g loosely packed fresh mint leaves

2 cups/25 g loosely packed cilantro leaves (see Dip Tip)

1 serrano chile, chopped

¼ cup/60 ml freshly squeezed lime juice

2 tbsp sugar

1 tsp ground cumin

1 tsp ground coriander

Fine sea salt

Place the coconut in a medium bowl and cover with hot tap water. Soak for 20 minutes. Drain, reserving the soaking liquid.

In a food processor or blender, combine the drained coconut, mint, cilantro, serrano, lime juice, sugar, cumin, coriander, and enough of the soaking liquid (about ¼ cup/60 ml) to encourage the ingredients to move around in the bowl. Process or blend, scraping down the sides of the bowl or carafe frequently, until the chutney becomes a smooth paste.

Transfer the chutney to a serving bowl or airtight container. Allow the chutney to sit at room temperature for at least 1 hour to allow the flavors to develop. Season with salt and store in an airtight container in the refrigerator for up to 1 week.

DIP TIP: A few cilantro stems in the chutney won't do any harm, but avoid any mint stems; they're much tougher and will have an adverse affect on the texture of the chutney.

126

FIGGY BOURBON CONSERVE

Figs grow in bumper crops here in the Pacific Northwest, and most folks with fig trees beg their neighbors to pick as many of the beautiful pod-shaped fruits as they can carry before they fall to the ground and make a sticky mess of their lawns.

This conserve was inspired by just such a picking foray. Instead of overdoing it with the sugar, like some fig jams, I like to focus on the deep, purple-brown flavor of figs, adding just a little bourbon and ginger to enhance the sensual flavor of the slow-stewed fruit. A natural partner for aged cheeses, this spread is great smeared with a little blue cheese, or try on the Brown Butter–Hazelnut Crackers (page 63) with a shaving of pecorino toscano for an unusual dessert nibble.

MAKES 1¾ CUPS/420 ML

1 lb/450 g ripe Mission figs

½ cup/100 g packed light brown sugar

¼ cup/60 ml bourbon

2 tbsp freshly squeezed lemon juice, plus
2 tsp finely grated organic lemon zest

1 tbsp finely chopped peeled fresh ginger

Rinse and pat dry the figs. Cut the fruit into quarters and discard the stems. Place the figs, brown sugar, bourbon, lemon juice, lemon zest, and ginger in a medium saucepan. Bring to a simmer over medium heat; reduce the heat to low and cook, stirring frequently, until the mixture is thick and jammy, 30 minutes.

Cool the mixture until just warm to the touch. Blend with an immersion blender or transfer the mixture to a blender and blend until smooth. Transfer the conserve to an airtight container and keep in the refrigerator for up to 1 month.

127

BACON AND CARAMELIZED ONION JAM

This dip may sound over-the-top, but its roots are firmly planted in the French tradition of *rillettes*—meat cooked and preserved in its own fat to create spreadable pâté. That said, this decadent dip is definitely "dude food," too; it will be an instant hit at your next Super Bowl party or barbecue alongside Corn Bread Crisps (page 29), Macadamia Nut and Coconut Flour Club Crackers (page 73), or Soda Water Crackers with Alder Smoked Salt (page 26).

As with most recipes, the success here has a lot to do with the shopping. Be sure to use good-quality smoked bacon like Nueske's applewood smoked bacon (www.nueskes.com) for the best flavor. This recipe yields enough jam to share; it makes a great gift when packaged in pretty little jars tied with a pig-pink ribbon.

MAKES ABOUT 2 CUPS/480 ML

1 tbsp extra-virgin olive oil

12 oz/340 g center-cut smoked bacon (8 to 10 slices),
cut into 1-in/2.5-cm lengths

2 onions, thinly sliced through the root end

2 garlic cloves, thinly sliced

1 tsp ground cumin

⅛ tsp ground cloves

½ cup/120 ml chicken broth

½ cup/100 g packed light brown sugar

3 tbsp balsamic vinegar

Fine sea salt

Freshly ground black pepper

128

Heat the olive oil in a large Dutch oven over medium heat. Add the bacon and cook, stirring frequently, until all the fat has rendered and the bacon is crisp, 10 to 12 minutes. Turn off the heat and transfer the bacon to a small bowl. Leave 2 tbsp of the drippings in the pan, reserve the rest for another use, or discard.

Add the onions to the pan and cook over medium-low heat, stirring occasionally, until the onions turn light caramel brown and have softened and broken down to about half their original volume, 15 to 20 minutes. If the onions begin to burn, reduce the heat, and be patient: it's crucial to cook down the onions slowly without burning them so they are sweet instead of bitter.

Reduce the heat to low if it is not already there and add the garlic, cumin, and cloves to the pan. Cook until the garlic becomes fragrant, about 2 minutes. Add the broth and bring to a simmer, scraping up the browned bits on the bottom of the pan. Cook, stir-ring constantly, until the broth has been absorbed, 4 minutes.

Add the cooked bacon and brown sugar. Cook, stirring constantly, until the mixture is syrupy, 5 minutes. Set aside and let the mixture cool for 10 minutes. Transfer the mixture to a food processor, add the vinegar, and process until the bacon is in pieces no larger than ½ in/12 mm and the onions are the consistency of marmalade, 10 one-second pulses. Season the mixture with salt and pepper and transfer to a serving bowl or airtight container. Serve at room temperature, or store in the refrigerator for up to 1 week. Reheat gently before serving.

129

WARM OLIVE TAPENADE
WITH PRESERVED LEMON

Cold olives leave me cold. You can marinate them, stuff them, or purée them into a tapenade, but if they're cool, I'm bored to tears. Warm olives are another matter. Applying just a little heat to olives transforms them into a fruity, sensuous pleasure.

For this warm olive tapenade, I use a mix of meaty, bright green Castelvetrano olives (find them at olive bars or in jars at better markets) and brinier kalamata olives to achieve a balance of sweet, salty, fruity, and bitter flavors.

This warm dip goes splendidly with the Caesar's Sablés (page 48, pictured opposite), the Smoked Almond Thins (page 62), and the buttery Macadamia Nut and Coconut Flour Club Crackers (page 73). It can be stored in the refrigerator for up to 2 weeks, so it's a great homemade holiday gift; consider making a double batch so you can share the warm olive love.

MAKES 1½ CUPS/360 ML

1 cup/160 g pitted Castelvetrano green olives

½ cup/80 g pitted kalamata black olives

2 tbsp extra-virgin olive oil

1 shallot, finely chopped

1 garlic clove, finely chopped

1 tsp chopped fresh thyme

1 tbsp finely chopped preserved lemon

130

In a food processor, pulse all the olives until they form a chunky paste the consistency of granola, or mound them on a cutting board and chop with a sharp chef's knife.

In a small sauté pan, heat the olive oil over medium heat. Add the shallot, garlic, and thyme and sauté until the shallot is tender and the garlic is fragrant but not browned, 1 minute. Add the chopped olives and preserved lemon and cook, stirring frequently, until the olives are hot to the touch, 3 minutes. Transfer the tapenade to a serving bowl and serve immediately. (Once cool, the tapenade can be stored in the refrigerator in an airtight container for up to 2 weeks. Rewarm in a small saucepan or in the microwave before serving.)

(DON'T TELL THEM IT'S VEGAN) MUSHROOM AND CASHEW PÂTÉ

Vaguely reminiscent of the mushroom pâtés served in the hippie era, this flavorful spread tastes much more sophisticated thanks to a mix of mushrooms (shiitake and portobello), fresh herbs, and a whiff of truffle oil. Be sure to scrape the black gills on the underside of the portobello mushrooms and discard them; the gills will turn the entire pâté an unattractive black color. For the best flavor, make this pâté a few hours in advance and serve it at room temperature or warm with Paper-Thin Semolina Cracker Sheets (page 45).

MAKES 1⅔ CUPS/405 ML

2 tbsp extra-virgin olive oil

1 onion, finely chopped

1 carrot, peeled and finely chopped

2 garlic cloves, finely chopped

8 oz/225 g portobello mushrooms, stems and black underside gills discarded, coarsely chopped

4 oz/110 g shiitake mushrooms, stems discarded, caps chopped

Kosher salt

⅓ cup/75 ml dry white vermouth or dry white wine

½ cup/60 g toasted cashews

1 tbsp finely chopped fresh Italian parsley

1½ tsp finely grated organic lemon zest

2 tsp fresh thyme leaves, chopped

1 tsp soy sauce

½ to 1 tsp white truffle oil

Freshly ground black pepper

132

In a large sauté pan, heat the olive oil over medium heat. When the oil is hot, add the onion and carrot and sauté until softened, 5 minutes. Add the garlic and cook for 30 seconds. Add the portobellos and shiitakes and a generous pinch of salt and sauté until the mushrooms have softened and have given off their liquid, 4 minutes. Add the vermouth and sauté, scraping up the browned bits from the bottom of the pan, until the liquid has nearly evaporated, 1 minute.

Transfer the mushroom mixture to a food processor. Add the cashews, parsley, lemon zest, thyme, and soy sauce. Process until smooth, scraping down the sides of the work bowl once or twice. Transfer the pâté to a microwave-safe bowl and allow the mixture to stand 1 hour to meld flavors. Reheat in the microwave until warm, add ½ tsp of the truffle oil, and season with salt and pepper. Taste and add more truffle oil if desired. The pâté can be made up to 3 days in advance and kept in the refrigerator in an airtight container until ready to use. Microwave until warm before serving.

133

ST. JACK'S CHICKEN LIVER MOUSSE

There are dishes that cause me to lose all self-restraint. This rich, silky chicken liver mousse from Chef Aaron Barnett of the charming Lyon-style bistro St. Jack in southeast Portland is one of those dishes. I embarrass myself (and my husband) with moans of delight every time I order this version of the French classic. Chef Barnett serves his mousse with slices of crusty baguette, but the Perfect Crostini (page 90) or the Paper-Thin Semolina Cracker Sheets (page 45) are excellent, crispier options.

MAKES 1 CUP/240 ML

½ lb/225 g chicken livers

1 cup/240 ml milk

Fine sea salt

Freshly ground black pepper

2 tbsp vegetable oil

2 tbsp finely chopped shallots

1 garlic clove, finely chopped

1 tbsp honey

1 to 2 tbsp brandy

½ cup/120 ml heavy whipping cream

134

Start the mousse at least 6 hours and up to 1 day before you plan to serve it. In a medium nonreactive bowl, combine the chicken livers with the milk. Cover with plastic wrap and refrigerate for at least 5 hours and up to 1 day. Drain the livers and pat dry thoroughly with paper towels. Season the livers generously with salt and pepper; set aside.

Heat 1 tbsp of the vegetable oil in a medium sauté pan over medium heat. Add the shallots and garlic and sauté until the shallots are translucent and the garlic is fragrant but not browned, 2 minutes. Scrape the shallots and garlic into a small bowl and set aside.

Wipe out the sauté pan with a paper towel, add the remaining 1 tbsp oil to the pan, and return it to the stove over high heat. When the oil is very hot but not smoking, carefully add the chicken livers, reduce the heat to medium-high, and sear the livers until they are deeply browned, 2 to 3 minutes per side. (The livers will pop and spit quite a bit; if you have a splatter screen, now is a good time to put it to use.)

Return the shallot-garlic mixture to the pan along with the honey. Add 1 tbsp of the brandy, carefully tilt the pan to ignite the alcohol if you have a gas burner, or use a kitchen match if you have an electric burner, and cook until the flames subside and the liquid in the pan is reduced to a thick glaze, about 45 seconds.

Transfer the chicken liver mixture to a food processor. Add the cream and process until the mixture is smooth; it will look like thick cream of mushroom soup, but never fear, the mousse will firm up a bit as it cools. Use a rubber spatula to push the mixture through a fine-mesh sieve into a medium bowl. Taste and add the remaining brandy or season with salt and pepper, if desired. Refrigerate until completely chilled and then cover tightly with plastic wrap and store in the refrigerator for up to 5 days.

135

TRIESTE-STYLE CRAB GRATIN

All along the northeastern coast of Italy, there are delicious versions of this hot crab dip. I found my favorite in a minuscule candlelit trattoria nestled in the harbor of Trieste. Unlike American versions that include heavy doses of mayonnaise and cheese, Italians let the flavor of the main ingredient shine by pairing the crab with simple flavors—parsley, lemon, and, most notably, mashed potatoes. The use of potatoes in this hot dip may seem unusual, but they give the gratin a light, creamy texture that will leave your guests guessing and reaching for more dip!

Serve Trieste-Style Crab Gratin with neutral-flavored crackers like the Soda Water Crackers with Alder Smoked Salt (page 26) or the Smoked Almond Thins (page 62), or pair it with the Black Pepper Taralli (page 53).

MAKES 2½ CUPS/600 ML

1 russet potato, peeled and cut into 1-in/2.5-cm cubes

Fine sea salt

5 tbsp/75 ml heavy whipping cream

2 tsp finely grated organic lemon zest, plus
1 tbsp freshly squeezed lemon juice

2 tbsp finely chopped fresh Italian parsley

⅛ tsp freshly ground black pepper

3 tbsp unsalted butter

1 onion, finely chopped

1 garlic clove, finely chopped

6 oz/170 g Dungeness or blue crabmeat, picked over

½ cup/20 g fresh breadcrumbs (see Dip Tip)

1 tbsp extra-virgin olive oil

Place the potato cubes in a medium pot and cover with enough cold water to come 2 in/5 cm over the potatoes. Add 2 tsp salt and bring to a boil. Cook until the potatoes are fork-tender, about 14 minutes. Drain the potatoes, place them in a large bowl, and mash until smooth. Add the cream, lemon zest, lemon juice, parsley, and pepper and stir to combine; set aside.

Preheat the oven to 375°F/190°C/ gas 5. Coat a 3-cup/700-ml gratin dish with cooking spray. In a medium sauté pan, melt the butter over medium heat. Add the onion and sauté until it is translucent but not browned, 5 minutes. Add the garlic and sauté until fragrant, 45 seconds. Pour the onion mixture into the bowl with the mashed potatoes and stir well to combine. Gently fold the crabmeat into the potato-onion mixture and season with salt, if desired. Transfer the mixture to the gratin dish.

In a small bowl, combine the breadcrumbs with the olive oil. Spread the breadcrumb mixture over the top of the gratin. (The gratin can be prepared to this point up to 1 day in advance. Cover with plastic wrap and refrigerate until ready to bake.) Bake the gratin uncovered until the top is golden brown and the dip is bubbling around the edges, 30 to 35 minutes. Serve hot.

DIP TIP: Dried breadcrumbs (the kind that come in a can) are not interchangeable with fresh, springy breadcrumbs! To make fresh breadcrumbs, tear a sandwich roll (such as a Kaiser bun) into 1-in/2.5-cm pieces and pulse in a food processor until finely ground. One bun will make about 1¼ cups/65 g of crumbs. Keep any leftover crumbs in a sealable plastic bag in the freezer for future use; you'll thank yourself later.

137

ALBACORE TUNA TARTARE
WITH HIJIKI

There are few better foods to indulge in than wild albacore tuna caught off the Pacific Northwest coast between midsummer and early fall. The fish is milder than its larger bluefin and yellowtail brethren, with a pearly pink flesh that needs little more than a simple soy dressing to adorn it. It's so good raw it's a travesty that so much of the fish ends up packed into cans!

Because the albacore in this dip is raw, it's crucial to buy very fresh fish labeled "sashimi grade" for flavor's and safety's sake. Serve this Japanese-inspired tartare with Asian-style crackers like the Crispy Wonton Triangles (page 77) for an upscale appetizer or simply scoop it up with Vietnamese Shrimp Chips (page 87) for a midnight nosh.

MAKES ⅔ CUP/165 ML

2 tsp dried hijiki seaweed (see Dip Tip)

½ cup/120 ml water

8 oz/225 g sashimi-grade raw albacore tuna loin

½ serrano or jalapeño chile, finely chopped

1 green onion, finely chopped

1 tbsp finely grated peeled fresh ginger

1 tbsp soy sauce

1½ tsp lemon-infused olive oil or canola oil

1½ tsp dark (toasted) sesame oil

1 tsp finely grated organic lemon zest

2 pinches ground white pepper

138

In a small bowl, combine the hijiki and water and set aside for 30 minutes to soften. Meanwhile, freeze the tuna for 30 minutes to make it firmer and thereby easier to dice.

Drain the seaweed, chop it, and place it in a medium bowl. Slice the tuna against the grain into ¼-in-/6-mm-thick slabs. Stack a few slabs, cut them into ¼-in-/6-mm-wide strips, and then cut the strips crosswise to create small cubes of tuna about ¼ in/6 mm square or smaller. Repeat with all the tuna and place the diced fish in the bowl with the hijiki.

Add the serrano, green onion, ginger, soy sauce, olive oil, sesame oil, lemon zest, and white pepper and toss gently to combine. Allow the mixture to sit for 15 minutes before serving, to allow the flavors to develop. You can make the components for the tartare up to 1 day in advance. Keep the tuna mixture and the dressing in separate airtight containers in the refrigerator until almost ready to serve.

DIP TIP: Hijiki is a dark green, almost black, sea vegetable that comes dried in bags at Asian markets and some health foods stores. I adore hijiki because it adds a salty, mineral tang to salads and spreads like this one, and it lasts indefinitely in an air-tight container. If you can't find hijiki, substitute finely chopped nori seaweed sheets (the kind used in rolling sushi), adding them to the dip (dry) immediately before serving.

139

INDEX

141

142

143

YUM!